REDLANDS
in

WORLD WAR I

REDLANDS

in

WORLD WAR I

ANN CORDY DEEGAN, MARIA CARRILLO COLATO,
NATHAN D. GONZALES AND DON MCCUE

THE
History
PRESS

Published by The History Press
Charleston, SC
www.historypress.net

First published 2017

Manufactured in the United States

ISBN 9781467136099

Library of Congress Control Number: 2016953506

Notice: The information in this book is true and complete to the best of our knowledge. It is offered without guarantee on the part of the authors or The History Press. The authors and The History Press disclaim all liability in connection with the use of this book.

This book is dedicated to the women and men of Redlands who served at home, elsewhere in the United States and overseas during World War I. To the forty who gave their lives in service, we acknowledge their "supreme sacrifice" whether in combat or due to another cause. A thank-you is extended to all for their efforts to make this world a better place.

CONTENTS

PREFACE

This work started several years ago when historian Ann Deegan began to see names of Redlands-area men who gave their lives in World War I. Knowing that the 100th anniversary of the United States' entry into World War I would be April 6, 2017, it seemed appropriate to write a book about these people in time for the event. Things grew from there. Deegan invited the historians at A.K. Smiley Public Library to collaborate on the project. Don McCue, director of A.K. Smiley Public Library and a military historian, was deemed the appropriate person to cover the war overseas. Nathan D. Gonzales, library archivist, head of special collections and longtime Redlands historian, could give a unique perspective on the homefront. Maria Carrillo Colato, library associate archivist, had access to fascinating information about women in the war from Redlands who served outside the town. As Deegan began her research into the thirty-nine men and one woman who gave their lives, it became apparent that over eight hundred men in the Redlands area were drafted or enlisted and as many of their stories as possible should be included; thus, the draft and enlisted chapters became part of this book. The last chapter, on the postwar years, emerged through research into the reburials from overseas and memorial building that continued for many years.

This work is not an effort to retell the basic history of World War I but to highlight the contributions and fascinating stories of Redlands-area men and women. Just a few facts are needed to tie these stories into the larger context. Although World War I started in Europe during 1914, the United States did not enter it until April 6, 1917. Ours was a short—but traumatic—part of the war, ending on November 11, 1918, with the German armistice. Some returned from war refusing to tell all they had seen, others were interviewed by local newspapers and gave talks in the schools and to community groups and a small group would never be able to tell their stories due to their deaths during the war. Those who stayed home fought the war in their own ways, including through groups such as the Red Cross or bond drives.

Today, we are lucky to have access to the local newspapers and family letters and photographs within the archives of A.K. Smiley Public Library to find these personal stories. For space saving, we have abbreviated the *Redlands Daily Facts* newspaper as the *Facts* throughout this book. Additionally, after the war, there was an effort by the War Department to gather up the draft cards, questionnaires and other official documents so that in future years they could be used to understand what took place. We are also fortunate that so much of that material has survived for our use today. The reference list at the back of this book has been designed to let readers know the general type of information used to create this book and to help others continue this research. Additionally, copies of all chapters of this book with complete references are available in the archives of A.K. Smiley Public Library, as is a large data file ordered by name of the Redlands-area men and women who served. The provided index at the end of this book includes names of men and women from the Redlands area and locations of greatest interest to our readership. We hope that you will find these stories as fascinating and thought-provoking as we have.

ACKNOWLEDGEMENTS

All book royalties will go to A.K. Smiley Public Library, whose staff and trustees had the foresight to collect and preserve the history of Redlands, making it possible to provide so many of the photographs used in this work. Many families provided images and history to the authors in creating this work. Their willingness to share has made Redlands' history richer for all. We wish to acknowledge Zac and Cathy Avey; Marilyn Fair Burchill; Bob Clinton; Jim and Ardith James; Win Lombard; Anne Ouelette; Alison, Eric and Leighton Paul; Richard and Dorotha Putnam; Sharon Swan; Kathy Bethell Texter; Harold Wilson; and Lois Fair Wilson. Several institutions searched records for us, contributed images and assisted our research in other ways: Geoffrey Fournier, superintendent, Oise-Aisne American Cemetery, France; Angelo T. Munsel, superintendent, Suresnes American Cemetery, France; Sarah A. Herrmann, digital communications manager, American Battle Monuments Commission; Mike Edson, American Legion Post 106, Redlands; Hillside Memorial Park staff, Redlands; Michele Nielsen, archivist and alumni historian, University of Redlands; Lisa Crunk, photo archivist, Naval History and Heritage Command; Claire Marie Teeters, president of operations, Yucaipa Valley Historical Society; Jonathan Casey (museum archivist and research center manager), Dean Weltmer (volunteer) and Ron Magee (volunteer researcher), Edward Jones Research Center, National World War I Museum and Memorial, Kansas City, Missouri; Marianna Apostolakis and Amy Hague, reference staff,

Sophia Smith Collection, Smith College, Northampton, Massachusetts; Tim Noakes, public service manager, Green Library, Stanford University; Daniel Hartwig, Stanford University Archives; and Marlea D. Leljedal, U.S. Army Heritage and Education Center, Carlisle, Pennsylvania. Other individuals have contributed time and effort to making this work possible, including Ashley Bandy, Char Burgess, Juan Colato, Sam Irwin, Janice Jones, Charline Ketcherside, Todd Loza, Susan McCue and Mark Radeleff. A big thank-you is extended to Special Collections staff Katie Montemayor and Teresa Letizia for their tireless work in aiding with research and in keeping the archives running smoothly as the book was in progress. Finally, a posthumous acknowledgment is extended to Jim Deegan, husband of Ann Deegan, whose continued encouragement of the research needed for this work kept the project going in its initial phases and who unfailingly cheered on the book. A career military officer, Jim served in Vietnam with the Twenty-Eighth Infantry Regiment, First Infantry Division, which proudly bears the name the "Lions of Cantigny" in honor of their predecessors' bravery at Cantigny, France, in 1918.

All images are from the collections of the archives of A.K. Smiley Public Library unless otherwise noted.

THE WAR AT HOME

Y ou may say that I consider Redlands the most beautiful city I have seen in California" remarked William Jennings Bryan upon his visit in May 1918. Bryan, three times nominated for president of the United States and secretary of state during President Woodrow Wilson's first term, found himself in Redlands while on a patriotic speaking tour through Southern California in support of U.S. involvement in the Great War.

That a town less than forty years of age could be described in such a way was a testament to the vision of the earliest pioneers of Redlands. Redlands

Picturesque Redlands looking north from Redlands Heights, with the snowcapped peaks of the San Bernardino Mountains in the distance.

was first dreamed up by Edward Judson and Frank Brown, both originally Connecticut men, in 1881. The two met after settling in the eastern part of the San Bernardino Valley—about ten miles southeast of the city of San Bernardino and some sixty-five miles east of Los Angeles—in the 1870s. After a couple attempts at business ventures, the two turned toward real estate development and focused their sights on the barren, semiarid hills south of the Mill Creek Zanja, an irrigation ditch from Mill Creek, a tributary of the Santa Ana River northeast of the future town dug during the days of the California missions.

During the mid-1880s, their new "Red Lands Colony" gained steam, leading to incorporation as a city in late 1888. In the 1880s, the Civil War was not yet a distant memory—a number of early residents were war veterans and their families looking for a new life in the West. An active chapter of the Grand Army of the Republic, a veterans' organization for those who fought to preserve the United States, enjoyed success in Redlands, as did former Confederates who made Southern California their new home. Any Redlander who experienced America in the 1860s hoped never to see the horrors of such a war again.

By 1910, Redlands had gone from a town of only a few hundred to a city of more than ten thousand, transforming the dry hills into a spectacle of progress, horticulture and agriculture. Thanks to a guaranteed water supply, in part in the form of a reservoir at Bear Valley (later named Big Bear Lake), a fairly solid economy based on the production of the Washington navel orange and the ability to ship fruit on railroads across the country, Redlands thrived. The influx of new residents over the years established the community with important values, with the spirits of philanthropy and volunteerism paramount. Albert and Alfred Smiley, identical twin brothers who were educators turned resort owners, made Redlands their winter home beginning in 1890 when they were in their mid-sixties. They, with many other early residents, provided both the example and foundation for philanthropy, with gifts to the town like A.K. Smiley Public Library and organizations to help those in need like Associated Charities, later renamed Family Service Association of Redlands.

After the orange crop, the most important industry was the "tourist crop." Multiple transcontinental railroad routes to California ushered in the beginning of tourism for the state, and Redlands became one of the premier destinations for "snowbirds." Special tourist trains stopped in Redlands, and new hotels, like the massive Casa Loma Hotel built in 1896, catered to their every need.

Not only did tourists understand the attractiveness of visiting Southern California in winter, so, too, did wealthy Americans from the Northeast and northern Midwest. In Redlands, many of the wealthy elite, like Albert Cameron Burrage of Massachusetts and John Alfred Kimberly of Wisconsin, discovered they could buy five or ten (or more) acres of land, build or acquire a winter residence surrounded by orange groves and realize substantial return on their investment with the annual orange harvest. By the turn of the century, Redlands boasted, at least anecdotally, more millionaires per capita than any other city in California.

When war broke out in Europe in 1914, Redlanders were concerned but had pressing challenges at home. A disastrous freeze during the winter of 1913 destroyed the orange crop and many of the trees, causing a brief financial depression for the town and surrounding orange-growing districts. University of Redlands, founded by Northern Baptists only a few years earlier in 1907, came close to being a failed experiment when pledges of financial support from locals went unfulfilled.

Fortunately, the industry rebounded within a few years, and the orange was once again king. As the 1916 presidential election approached, Woodrow Wilson may have run with the slogan "He kept us out of war," but there were much more pressing issues on the minds of Redlands voters: Prohibition and the specter of war with Mexico as Pancho Villa and his troops wreaked havoc along the border.

Since before incorporation as a city, Redlands struggled with temperance and Prohibition. Among the first ordinances passed by the founding city council was one dealing with the regulation of spirituous beverages, and this remained the most controversial, divisive and consistent topic in local elections until the Eighteenth Amendment went into effect in 1920.

The uneasy situation with Mexico led to military effort on the part of the United States, and the impact for Redlands was made real when Redlands' Company G, part of the California National Guard, was mobilized as part of the response. This seemed a much more real challenge that affected local citizens more directly than war in Europe. That threat was finally mitigated in early 1917, and attention again turned to local matters.

With this as the backdrop heading toward the end of 1916, and with war continuing to rage in Europe, the philanthropic spirit of Redlanders began to kick into high gear and would prove to remain there through the events of 1917 and 1918. Seeing the turmoil faced by people of the Allied nations, a group of Redlanders formed the Allies War Relief Fund Committee. In November 1916, the group appealed to other like-minded citizens with

361

American
War Relief Committee
of France

Miss Schofield and Miss Fell will give
a lecture in behalf of the

ORPHANS OF FRANCE

Monday evening, February 12, at 8 o'clock
at the Contemporary Club House.

～～～ NO ADMISSION. ～～～

Do Not Circulate

A. B. SMILEY PUBLIC LIBRARY
REDLANDS, CALIFORNIA

After nearly three years of war in Europe, the need for assistance from people in the United States grew. Many programs related to war relief, like this one from February 12, 1917, were held in Redlands.

"An Appeal to the People of Redlands of British Ancestry." The group had already raised and distributed nearly $1,700 to the British Red Cross, the Over-Seas Club and funds for hospital supplies to France and now sought to raise yet more money. The "Appeal" offered up this plea: "Our kindred are willingly giving their lives to the cause, and the need is great, each month thousands of the bread winners of poor families are killed, more thousands are disabled for life, and now with the end not yet in sight, hundreds of thousands of homes are dependent on outside help."

As was true across the country in the months and years before Germany's policy of unrestricted submarine warfare in the Atlantic and the revelation of German attempts for Mexico to begin a military offensive into the United States, sympathy was found for those affected by war on both sides of the conflict. The Redlands German Relief Committee took the opportunity of Wilson's order for November 30 to be celebrated as "Thanksgiving Day… set aside as a day to give thanks, a day of feasting and joy, and a day to give to the poor and needy" to appeal for funds sent to widows and orphans of Germany. By early December 1916, more than $300 was raised and transmitted to Germany for relief.

Western Europe wasn't the only part of the world ravaged by the war. The Ottomans waged war in Syria and Armenia, and Redlands began raising funds for Armenian-Syrian relief in 1915. By April 1917, Redlanders contributed nearly $1,000 to that cause. While relief was an important component of philanthropy, it wouldn't compare to the outpouring of support that came with the United States' entry into the Great War in April 1917.

Redlanders supported the work of the Red Cross before the U.S. entry into the war by making hospital supplies and garments, but there was no official chapter in town. The events of April 1917 brought the issue to the fore, and an official chapter was formed, with the complete support of the Redlands City Council. Throughout the war, the Redlands chapter would undertake the work of caring for dependent soldiers' families, making supplies for hospitals, organizing classes in first aid and hygiene and raising money for the overall work of the American Red Cross. Immediately after the chapter's creation, a membership drive was launched, along with a financial campaign to raise $25,000 for the Red Cross War Fund (roughly $470,000 in 2016 dollars).

To raise the quota of funds, volunteers formed nine teams, each with a captain. Remarkably, the group met the goal the first week of July. "It was the spirit of Redlands that did it, and once we got started, nothing could stop us. Redlands is not yet through giving, for as long as our boys keep going to the front, so long will Redlands want to contribute to the Red Cross Fund," remarked fund drive coordinator Theodore Doan of the Red Cross.

Indeed, it was. When Redlands' Company G was mobilized once again, this time in April 1917, with the aim of aiding the Allies in Europe, the war came home in ways it hadn't until that point. Among the early projects of the Redlands Red Cross was the creation of "comfort bags" for Company G men at camp. The Military Relief Committee of the local Red Cross urged women to create the bags, into which items like needles, thread, buttons, toilet articles and other items would be placed. The committee provided the material for the bags, the sewing pattern and the contents. By mid-July, one hundred bags were completed, with the addition of shoelaces

The Redlands chapter of the American Red Cross found a home in the Academy of Music building at Orange Street and Citrus Avenue.

contributed by a local business, Bennet Bros. Seventy-five of the bags were sent to Company G, which was training at North Island, San Diego, with the remaining twenty-five saved for future recruits to the company.

The local Red Cross found office space in the Academy of Music building, at the northwest corner of Orange Street and Citrus Avenue, from which to conduct operations. At the same time, the chapter began to organize classes in fields like first aid. The first-aid class partnered with the Redlands Young Women's Christian Association to provide space for the twenty students in their five-week class that met twice a week.

In addition to classes on first aid and nursing, Redlanders had the opportunity to help fulfill the need for hospital supplies in Europe. That July, the group appealed to local women to help create these supplies, a task they would be asked to fulfill throughout the remainder of the war. In the first delivery of supplies came sheeting and the material for making bandages, as well as pre-cut fabric for hospital shirts and pajamas to be sewn. A great advantage to volunteers was that the components could be taken home for completion. Yarn for knitting socks, mufflers, helmets and mittens was expected soon, as well as cotton for eye bandages and swabs, material for pillowcases and gauze. The volunteers worked diligently over the coming months. In March 1918 alone, 26,600 gauze compresses, 18,275 four-tail bandages, 702 pairs of socks, 185 handkerchiefs, 145 bed shirts and 121 sweaters, among thousands of other items, were made and shipped from Redlands. The total that month was nearly 50,000 items.

Over the course of the remainder of the war, numerous civic organizations hosted fundraisers to benefit the Red Cross, from fraternal lodges and youth organizations to women's clubs. Redlands Country Club even worked to support the Red Cross in its own way: when the golf season opened on December 1, 1917, a new sweepstakes was instituted for members who wished to participate. A one-cent cash penalty per stroke for every stroke beyond the player's handicap on eighteen holes realized twenty-five dollars the first day.

Another way the chapter worked to raise funds was through a secondhand shop of donated goods, which opened just in time for the holiday season in mid-November 1917. The *Facts* advertised, "There is no collection of riff-raff, but a great variety of articles of beauty as well as usefulness. The case of silver is one of the principal attractions, full of pieces that will make most desirable Christmas present[s]. The quality of dresses shown will be a surprise—also the number of fur pieces.…The ten-cent table presents values that beat the Woolworth stores."

In early May 1918, the American Red Cross launched its Second Red Cross War Fund drive. Each area was given a quota to raise, and the quota for Redlands was $12,000. "I feel that the people of this city should greatly exceed this amount, and I am confident that we will go 'over the top' in a magnificent manner," remarked Eldridge M. Lyon, chairman of the campaign committee. Lyon, a leading citizen in Redlands, was a successful orange grower, civic leader and philanthropist and a longtime trustee of Smiley Library. The structure of the campaign was similar to the first drive, with teams assigned to canvass every part of town. By the end of the month, the group not only went "over the top," a popular phrase to establish the goal of a fundraising campaign that exceeded expectation, but also raised nearly $28,000—more than double the quota. Of the total, $21,000 was in cash, a remarkable accomplishment during a time when demands for financial contributions came in many forms.

Once war was declared, President Wilson and Congress had to find ways to actually pay for it. The U.S. military was a relatively modest peacetime force, and even though the policy of preparedness had begun to increase the ranks

Redlanders mounted parades and rallies to support the Red Cross and other war-related causes throughout 1917–18. This Red Cross car is on Colton Avenue at Orange Street.

The business center of Redlands, State Street looking east from Fourth. The three-story building at the far left is the Redlands National Bank at Orange Street.

and expenditures for supplies, it could not be enough for requirements of full-scale war. At the beginning of May 1917, the Liberty Loan was announced in Redlands, with the goal of the federal government to sell $2 billion in bonds across the country to fund the war effort. Redlands National Bank placed an advertisement in the *Facts* on May 4, 1917, in support of the loan. "America has thrown her lot with the Allies. The honor of America is at stake. The war must be financed, and each man and woman and child in the United States must bear a portion of the load." Of course, this was also a good opportunity for banks to demonstrate their patriotism while soliciting new customers. All of the Redlands banks got into the spirit, sometimes placing joint ads for Liberty Bonds. The very first day, Redlanders subscribed to more than $13,000 in the bonds, which paid 3.5 percent. On May 23, a special committee to increase interest in the Liberty Loan was appointed by the general headquarters in San Francisco, led by the presidents of the local banks. In addition, the newspapers volunteered to "patriotically give space to bring the matter to the attention of the public."

A few days later, a quota to raise $150,000 was designated by the committee in consultation with a representative of the Federal Reserve Bank. "A bond battalion, armed to the teeth with the right kind of financial patriotism, will invade the city of Redlands during the next few weeks and besiege every closely guarded purse in the city. They are a ruthless lot and the only terms of peace they will consider are generous subscriptions to the Liberty Loan," reported the *Facts*. The City of Redlands subscribed $5,000 from its funds, while numerous individuals, families and businesses also got in on the action. Two weeks later, it was announced that more than $165,000 was already pledged to the bonds, the lowest amount being $50. The *Facts* even reported that part-time resident Albert C. Burrage subscribed to $500,000 of bonds through the Boston drive.

As the war ground on in Europe in 1917, it became clear that the $2 billion from the Liberty Loan was not enough, and a second national loan program was announced in October. The new committee met at the Redlands Chamber of Commerce and selected Arthur Isham, longtime secretary of the chamber, as secretary, and Jennie Davis, a leading woman in social and philanthropic circles, was added to the committee to coordinate the solicitation drive with women's organizations—the Contemporary Club in particular. The Contemporary Club was founded in 1894 and, in the nearly twenty years of its existence, had become a great force for women, complete with a large clubhouse across the street from Smiley Library at Vine and Fourth Streets. Local church ministers were also brought into the mix, and they agreed to speak in support of the loan from their pulpits on Sunday, October 14.

A week later, $85,000 was raised through the sale of the bonds to locals. Jennie Davis reported that the Contemporary Club's committee had secured more than $30,000 in subscriptions. A shift in tactics also entered the mix: peer pressure. The *Facts* reported, "The Liberty Loan campaign will come to a climax in Redlands next Wednesday afternoon when every man who is able to buy a bond and has not will be rounded up and convinced that it his patriotic duty to do so and to subscribe an amount proportionate to his financial status." For that "climax" on October 24, an event was also planned downtown, featuring the Municipal Band and local speakers talking about the bonds.

The night before the "climax" event, a large crowd gathered at Redlands High School for a bonfire in support of the bond campaign, and Redlanders who had "a piece of historic or imported wood, a relic or an heirloom they are willing to sacrifice [were] asked to bring the same and place it on the fire." The Municipal Band was also on hand, playing patriotic music throughout the evening. The following day, there was a large turnout at the rally held on East State Street. By the time the drive ended on October 26, Redlands citizens and businesses subscribed to $298,100 worth of liberty bonds, quite an achievement for a city of ten thousand.

Among the positive work to raise funds for organizations like the Red Cross and the war work of YMCA and YWCA, there were also more challenging sides to life. In order to try to unify the American people against Germany and the Central powers, a powerful propaganda machine was created to make Germans into a hurtful enemy. Even though as of 1910 only 178 residents of Redlands were born in Germany, and 80 were born in Austria (0.026 percent of Redlands' population), anyone could be a spy working covertly for Germany. On April 17, 1917, eleven days after the U.S. declaration of war against Germany passed Congress, the announcement was made that resident aliens in Redlands must surrender any firearms, ammunition or munitions in their possession to the city marshal. A receipt was given so that the property could be claimed after the war. Any "alien enemy who fails to surrender such articles within twenty-four hours after public notice…will be subject to summary arrest if such articles shall be found in his possession."

Even though patriotism ran high with the declaration of war, the work of the Red Cross and the first Liberty Loan fund drive, the war still seemed a far-off reality—until the beginning of the draft in the summer of 1917. An editorial in the *Facts* remarked, "We have not been altogether conscious of the war, up to this time, but that consciousness is being borne into the hearts and minds of these young men and their immediate families, at least, as well as to those who have volunteered." Early on, the newspaper took a very prowar position, publishing articles like "Who's Who among the Pacifists" in order to discredit those who spoke with the hope of some kind of peaceful solution or who continued with a more isolationist point of view. In his commencement address given to graduates at University of Redlands in 1917, Reverend Charles Edward Locke of Los Angeles said, "The sentiments of the pacifist are dangerous, incendiary, disloyal and traitorous. No matter how they are uttered or by whom they are exploited, even if by those who are shielded by the robes of the church, they are treason." Articles also discussed German propaganda and worked to justify U.S. involvement in the war. One editorial wrote that "above all else [Germany] must be beaten because victory for Germany would mean the triumph of brutal barbarism over civilization, and abandonment of the principles vital to the life of America—'government of the people, by the people, for the people.' Is it not then the war of every American, the war of every man wherever he may be found with the wish for free pursuit of life and happiness?" Another article asserted, "Any peace that is possible now is equivalent to German victory" in October 1917.

Some Redlanders certainly became entranced with anti-German sentiment. Aaron Leipsic, who owned a clothing store on State Street for many years, fell victim to rumors that questioned his loyalty. The situation was so distressing that he took out a lengthy ad on the front page of the September 6, 1917 issue of the *Facts*. "To the People of Redlands: There have come to my knowledge within the past few days reports that I have been guilty of making unpatriotic, even treasonable statements.…I have never made any statement in any way, shape or form favoring Germany in the present conflict, since the United States has been at war. I am a native of California, born in the city of San Francisco.…I have lived in Redlands nearly all of my business life.…I brand the statements that have been made about me as viciously false."

In a more amusing situation, George van der Linda, owner of the Holland Grocery in Redlands, ordered supplies for his store, which arrived addressed to George *von* der Linda. Being a native of the Netherlands but a naturalized citizen of the United States for twenty-five years, he took offense at the "Germanization" of his name and refused the shipment.

January 1918 saw a new ruling from the War Department requiring cities of five thousand inhabitants or more register male German aliens living there. Police were directed to secure a photograph, a complete description and fingerprints. At the time, Redlands did not have the equipment to take fingerprints, so it had to be procured. By January 25, the order was expanded to require that all "enemy aliens" register or be liable for internment during

Redlanders showed patriotism in numerous ways, like the song "That's What We'll Raise with Germany" by Frank Cook and Carroll Higbey, published in Redlands.

the war. The term "enemy alien" was defined as "all natives, citizens, denizens or subjects of a foreign nation or government with which war has been declared, being males of the age fourteen years and upward, who shall be within the United States and not actually naturalized as American citizens." An April decision expanded registration requirements to include women defined as "alien enemies," too.

The 1917–18 academic year at Redlands High School canceled the beginning-level German language class because of a lack of demand, although advanced classes continued because of students who had studied it in previous years. The school announced in May 1918 that no German-language class would be taught in the fall of that year, as it was being removed from the curricula of schools around the country. Fortunately, Mary Lombard, the teacher, remained on the faculty because she also taught Spanish and French.

Those issues aside, Redlands made concerted efforts to support the war goals in every way it could, even while daily life continued along normal paths. Tourism and business still operated as important aspects of the local economy. Movie houses showed patriotic films like *The Kaiser: Beast of Berlin*, *Over There* and *Pershing's Crusaders*. The Harris Company department store sold khaki-colored yarn for knitting sweaters and socks. Hutchins, a confectioner on West State Street, even sold "Liberty Candies."

Being an agricultural economy, Redlands made great strides for the war effort in that arena. As soon as war was declared in 1917, agricultural resources mobilized in order to increase the food supply so that foodstuffs could make their way to Europe. City government asked individuals interested in farming to plant tomatoes and potatoes in vacant lots and fallow lands around town. With an ear toward supporting the food effort, Redlander Mildred Wheat composed the song "I'm Raising Vegetables for Uncle Sam," which proved to be very popular in town and sold well at the Adams Music store. Redlands women did the best they could with food rationing, including designated meatless days, flourless days and limited amounts of sugar. Smiley Library even distributed "Food Conservation Pledge Cards" for residents to demonstrate their willingness to support the conservation program. Demonstrations on how to help conserve food were given at the 1918 National Orange Show and at the Contemporary Club. Everyone could help the war effort in some way.

Smiley Library, too, found ways to support the war effort. In addition to adding titles to the circulating collection that highlighted war themes, the library undertook a campaign to gather donated books and magazines

Some One at the Front Is Fighting for You

BACK HIM UP
by giving him Good Books and Magazines

THE PUBLIC LIBRARY
will send them for you

The American Library Association partnered with A.K. Smiley Public Library for donations of books and magazines to send to military camps and cantonments.

to send to training camps. An August 1917 headline for an article on the topic proclaimed "Send Books to Soldiers and Help Pass the Tedious Time—Library Will Receive Them." More than five hundred books found their way to the library for the soldiers during that drive. The following October, the American Library Association called on the library to raise $400 for the War Library Fund, which provided libraries for soldiers in cantonments and serving overseas. When the campaign closed on October 15, leaders expressed confidence that the drive was successful. Throughout the remainder of the war, the library participated in additional collections of books for soldiers, with thousands sent from Redlands.

Liberty bonds weren't the only way the federal government expected Redlanders to support the war effort financially. In December 1917, the post office received its first supply of war savings stamps and thrift stamps, part of a new campaign to raise another $2 billion. Buyers of war savings stamps, which began at $4.12 each and increased one cent each month during 1918, affixed them to a war savings certificate, which had space for twenty stamps.

Hundreds of books donated for soldiers near the circulation desk of Smiley Library.

The U.S. Treasury guaranteed $5.00 redemption for each stamp, beginning on January 1, 1923. Thrift stamps, on the other hand, appealed to those with smaller amounts to lend, like children. The value of thrift stamps was $0.25 but bore no interest. A thrift stamp certificate held space for sixteen stamps and had no cash value, but it could be redeemed for a war savings stamp when presented along with the difference between $4.00 and the value of a war savings stamp.

The local WSS committee selected Arthur Isham from the chamber of commerce as its secretary, with past mayor Jacob J. Suess as chairman. The committee sought to leave no coinage in Redlands unchanged for stamps, with drives organized through churches, schools and clubs, in addition to soliciting individuals. In January 1918, Isham sought assistance from Reverend Nathan Hynson, pastor at the First Presbyterian Church, to coordinate the effort for houses of worship. Isham desired to "communicate with you on the subject of presenting the work of the war saving stamp propaganda in the churches." Over the next several months, the committee organized rallies, meetings and savings drives to encourage Redlanders to

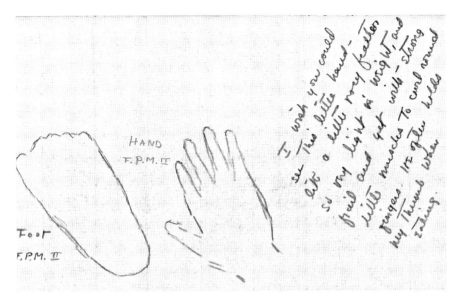

Laurence Morrison was serving in France when his wife, Margaret, gave birth to their son Frank P. Morrison II. Margaret included these sketches in a letter on July 2, 1918.

purchase both war savings stamps and thrift stamps. In June, Suess remarked that "the purchase of War Savings Stamps is a solemn duty no loyal citizen can afford to ignore. These stamps are as much a part of the great war machine as the shot and shell fired from the big guns of the American sector by our boys in France."

The thrift stamp campaign committee targeted schoolchildren because of the smaller investment required to purchase a thrift stamp. The *Facts* encouraged friendly competition between elementary schools with weekly totals of stamp sales. Kingsbury School was the clear winner in June 1918, with $3,016.18 in stamp sales, followed by McKinley school at $1,650.94. The total raised to that point by all six local elementary schools stood at just shy of $7,000.00, an outstanding showing

Redlands set its quota for WSS at $165,000, but by November 1, 1918, it had only reached $100,000. Coupled with the third and fourth liberty bond campaigns, Redlanders seemed weary of all the myriad expectations of fundraising.

The nation's third liberty loan campaign kicked off in April 1918, aiming to raise billions more for the war effort. The local effort sought to broaden support for the campaign by creating a women's committee with Jennie Davis as chairperson. "California women are to be put on record for citizenship according to the manner in which they qualify in the third Liberty Loan campaign," wrote the *Facts*, a not-so-veiled reference to the women's suffrage movement in the United States, which had yet to achieve the Nineteenth Amendment to the Constitution granting the right to vote in federal elections.

Charles M. Brown, a major figure in the orange-growing arena, served as chairman of the Liberty Loan Committee. By April 11, the committee had raised nearly $250,000 for the bonds, more than half the $412,000 quota for the town. Part of the campaign included a button the purchaser received with the first bond. The committee encouraged bondholders to wear their pins, so that "the effect on the 'Bond Slackers' will be noticeable, as they will feel pretty uncomfortable until they, too, display a button. The Liberty Bond flags should also be displayed in the stores and homes of the city as were the Red Cross flags at Christmas time."

To boost support, the committee arranged for soldiers from Redlands to return home from Camp Kearny the weekend of April 20 to participate in a liberty loan demonstration at the Municipal Amphitheater in Smiley Park, the site of the future Redlands Bowl. Demonstrating patriotism, a number of Redlanders contributed money to pay for the requisite train tickets, even though the soldiers were not related to them. A week later, officials announced that Redlands was "over the top" in subscriptions, and by May 4, more than

The municipal flagpole stood at the Triangle, an island of land created by the intersection of Orange Street, Citrus Avenue and Cajon Street. This photo looks north on Orange Street, with the Triangle at the left.

$500,000 was subscribed. The national Loan Committee provided Redlands with a "Liberty Loan Honor Flag" that city officials hoisted on the large municipal flagpole at the Triangle, a small triangular island created by the intersection of Orange Street, Cajon Street and Citrus Avenue, during a large ceremony on May 6.

Because of the success of the third loan, the committee for the fourth liberty loan tasked Brown to chair the next campaign that August. Positive developments on the western front contributed to spirited fundraising. Businesses even got in on the action, promoting the bond drive. The Harris Company store on State Street asked Redlanders to loan photographs of soldiers and sailors for use in store displays for the duration of the campaign. To increase excitement, a special train carrying war relics, the Mare Island Marine Band and special speakers on a tour through Southern California arrived in Redlands on the evening of September 30. More than 3,700 Redlanders passed through the cars on the train while it sat at the Southern Pacific depot downtown, and the parade and program at the amphitheater created quite the fervor for the liberty loan.

The campaign worked on the peer-pressure model in even more direct ways with the fourth loan. The *Facts* admonished, "This is the final notice to all citizens who have not done their duty. We will start publishing names… next week….Remember that a man whose name is published in the slacker

Children of the Pray family play as World War I soldier and nurses at the Pray home on the Terrace at Church Street. The service flag bears three blue stars and one gold star to honor the loss of Joseph Pray. *Courtesy of the Pray family.*

list will have no standing in the state or the nation. His leaving Redlands will avail him naught; it will follow him. A slacker will never live long enough to live down his deserved reputation….He will never live long enough to overcome his treasonable actions." Fortunately, Redlanders were able came forward and subscribed to the loan. Albert Burrage even sent $25,000 to support the Redlands campaign. Redlands once again went "over the top" with the loan drive, with a record $820,000 in liberty loan subscriptions.

Patriotism remained a strong and predictable theme for myriad events in 1917, including Memorial Day, Flag Day and Independence Day. As the war continued, and more of Redlands' own left for training and service overseas, patriotism reached a fever pitch. On March 15, 1918, a mass meeting was held at city hall to discuss the proposition of a pageant for Redlands. Lillian Burkhart Goldsmith, who had experience with other pageants in Southern California, felt that "a pageant at this time should be made applicable to the community, but patriotic in nature." Voices for and against the proposition were raised, with equally prominent men and women on both sides of the question. By the end of the meeting, a committee was appointed to solicit the funds needed to produce a real pageant.

Planning commenced apace, and by the end of March, *Son of the Red Lands* was selected as the title, April 20 selected as the date and the structure of the event sketched out. Several well-known operatic actresses from Los Angeles, as well as "women prominent in the civic, club and social life of California" were selected to take part. The University of Redlands Glee Club, local Boy Scouts and numerous men and women were also tapped to participate.

Advertising cards were given not only to local businesses but also to businesses in surrounding communities like San Bernardino, Riverside, Hemet and San Jacinto. The Southern Pacific and Santa Fe Railroads offered special rates to Redlands from all points south of Santa Barbara for the pageant. Hotels prepared for the arrival of hundreds of guests, banners were erected in town and residents were encouraged to write to friends and family about the spectacular event. The Saturday before the pageant was designated as a cleanup day in Redlands. "Owing to the pageant with its thousands of out-of-town visitors the Chamber of Commerce has decided that the annual Redlands Clean-Up Day shall be held on Saturday, April 13. Every citizen of Redlands is expected to co-operate in making the city as attractive as possible," wrote William P. Burke, chairman of the Redlands Chamber of Commerce Health and Sanitation Committee. On the day of the event, the Automobile Club of Southern California placed signs on the roads from Los Angeles to Redlands, directing travelers to the town.

April 20 proved to be a pinnacle of patriotism. The committee organized a rally at the Municipal Amphitheater for the third liberty loan, and all businesses closed from 2:00 to 3:00 p.m. At 8:00 p.m., the pageant finally began. The *Facts* described the pageant's opening splendor:

> *Myriad twinkling stars shone through a fiery streaked sky as if Old Glory "o'er the ramparts we watched" held out a message of human hope when three thousand men and women of Redlands and Southern California gasped their amazement at the electric beauty of Redlands' first annual pageant at the municipal amphitheater. It was as if the banner which heralded the fact of freedom of men had once more raised its proud stars and stripes above the smoke of battle, signaling the imminence of liberty in every land under the sun.*

The pageant appeared in three acts. The first, "The Garden of Make Believe," depicted the land of fairies and glow worms. Act II, "The Legend of the Arrow Head," told a story of Native Americans in the valley and depicted the fulfillment of a prophecy when a white child settler is held up before them. Act III began with a series of allegorical dances, followed by the segment depicting the war. The child from Act II appeared as the "Son of the Red Lands" opposite the figure of war. Individuals playing the parts of Hope, Love, Knowledge, Freedom, Peace and Democracy were featured in scenes, and finally Mary Kimberly Shirk appeared as the Goddess of Liberty. Shirk was the daughter of John Alfred and Helen Cheney Kimberly, who had retired to Redlands after founding and running the successful Kimberly Clark Company of paper products, and was visiting her parents while her husband, Elbert Shirk, served in the U.S. military overseas.

The pageant was so successful that it was mounted again a month later, this time in Los Angeles. The name was changed to *Son of the Southland* to broaden its appeal. The *Los Angeles Times* reported, "Probably the greatest crowd that has ever assembled in the bounds of Los Angeles gathered last evening at Exposition Park to witness the gigantic pageant-masque *The Son of the Southland*. They came by tens of thousands from every direction."

The War Department continued training new troops as more and more men entered the service. War tends to accelerate technological advances for the purpose of obtaining an edge over the enemy, and World War I was no exception. This war was the first time the United States engaged in one particular technological advance: the airplane. In order to have an effective air corps, pilots must be trained.

For some of the same reasons that the movie industry located in Southern California, so, too, did the War Department select the region for a new aviation training school. The site chosen was in nearby Alessandro, an area southwest of Redlands and southeast of Riverside. The *Facts* boasted, "The station…is said to be climatically and topographically perfect." The Redlands Chamber of Commerce immediately jumped on the opportunity to promote Redlands, suggesting to the commanding officer at the camp that Redlands hotels could accommodate staff and workmen for the camp and would provide transportation to and from the camp in just forty-five minutes. At the same time, the chamber sought to compile a list of workmen from Redlands who were interested in employment at the camp, anticipating that as many as one hundred might be called.

Work began by mid-March, and the Southwestern Home and Telephone Company of Redlands was awarded the contract to build a telephone system for the camp. Construction of the initial buildings and runway was completed very quickly. On June 4, the first airplane left March Field, the new name for the camp, and landed in Redlands near the intersection of Colton Avenue and Judson Street, east of the university. Students from March Field created a great attraction on August 1, when six planes landed in town—the largest number of planes ever seen in Redlands at one time. Numerous locals came out to see the excitement the landings created.

Construction of March Field so close to Riverside created serious concerns for some in that city. Many believed that the mobilization of large numbers of young men attracted its own set of nuisances, as well as businesses that cater to them with specialized services. Riverside's city council soon attempted to take preemptive action to protect its population and passed an ordinance "to better protect the public morals by providing for the licensing of hotels and rooming houses, by prohibiting the occupancy of hotels, rooming houses, buildings and residences by lewd women and prostitutes, and by prohibiting certain acts and things that might tend to produce immorality, and by declaring certain things nuisances and providing penalties and for other purposes." In the first draft, Section XI read "It shall be unlawful for persons to indulge in caressing, hugging, fondling, embracing, spooning, kissing, etc., while in or upon or about or near any of the streets, walks, drives, parks or other public places in the City of Riverside."

News of the "Anti-Kissing Law" of Riverside spread all over Southern California and doubtless even farther, including to headlines in Redlands. By the first meeting of Redlands' city council the following June, it was a topic on people's minds. On June 5, the *Facts* headline proclaimed, "Redlands

University of Redlands students dedicated the 1917–18 yearbook *La Letra* to students serving in the military.

Is to Have an Anti-Kissing Law in Near Future," and the following day, the headline in the *Redlands Review* read, "Anti-Kissing Law for Redlands." Surprisingly, with little or no public discussion, the potential ordinance for Redlands was quietly dropped. Even though the *Facts* wrote that the city council directed the city attorney to draft a preliminary ordinance for the next council meeting, it never surfaced.

As summer looked toward the fall of 1918, even with great advances made by the Allies in Europe, training remained of paramount importance. A number of men from the University of Redlands either enlisted or were drafted in 1917 and 1918, which affected the size of the student body. As did many churches and fraternal organizations, the university dedicated a service flag in honor of the students who had left in the service of the country. Pi Chi, the first fraternity at Redlands, displayed its service flag in December 1917, with eighteen stars, one for each member serving. The following day, the university's flag debuted with forty-nine stars. More would be added as students left to serve. The war provided an opportunity, however, for the university to aid the country while securing new students. The possibility of military instruction and the creation of a government-sponsored Student Army Training Corps (SATC) on campus was the answer. Coach Ashel Cunningham took a six-week training course at the Presidio army base in San Francisco beginning in August 1918 to learn how to drill students. University president Victor Duke understood well the advantages of such a program to bring more male students to the campus, as did the chamber of commerce, which became an important booster of the program.

By September 18, 125 students had enrolled in the SATC, and the number had swelled to 150 by September 30. Because of the program, the total enrollment at the university for the fall term was nearly double what it was the previous year. A new barracks was built to house some of the SATC students at the east end of the athletic field. The SATC group was organized into a daily military-style schedule, beginning with assembly at 6:10 a.m., drill at 6:25 a.m., breakfast at 6:45 a.m. and various classes, assemblies and inspections throughout the day, Saturdays included. "Taps" was played nightly at 10:00 p.m. Of the 150 who enrolled, only 128 ended up as inductees for the SATC program. Still, it was a marked increase in the overall enrollment that the university desperately needed to survive.

An error in reporting from the United Press wire precipitated the headline "War Is Over—Germany Signs Armistice" on November 7, 1918. Redlands greeted this news with great excitement, and a spontaneous parade formed

Young Men's Christian Association.
Sixth St. and Citrus Ave.

Redlands, California, December, 7, 1918.

Dear Friend:

We wish to take this opportunity to thank you for your recent subscription to the Y. M. C. A. We are now serving, directly, over two hundred boys, one hundred and thirty S. A. T. C. men and approximately sixty men of this community. We will give a three months membership to each returned soldier throughout the coming year. We would very much appreciate a personal visit from you.

Sincerely,
FRED L. DYE, Secretary.

Above: Even though the war was over, the Redlands YMCA continued to support members of the University of Redlands's Student Army Training Corps, as well as returning soldiers.

Opposite, top: Stanley Morrison sports an Imperial German Pickelhaube helmet souvenir in Redlands after the war.

Opposite, bottom: Laurence Morrison holds son Frank after returning from France.

at the Elks Club on West State Street, led by the Municipal Band. The group marched north on Orange and then back down to the Triangle. Dignitaries delivered impromptu speeches to the assembled crowd. Unfortunately, the war was not, in fact, over.

Five days later, on November 11, 1918, the warring nations signed the armistice. News traveled to Redlands about 1:00 a.m. on the eleventh, when the *Facts* reported that "even the soundest sleepers in Redlands were made aware…that the armistice had been signed. The news was received about 1 o'clock and immediately whistles were blown and bells rung. Both trucks of the fire department were taken out and raced through the streets, the giant sirens informing everyone of the glad tidings." Celebrations continued through the night and into the day. At 3:00 p.m., a parade formed at the Elks lodge, again led by the Municipal Band. The procession included the sixty-six draftees who were to have left for training that day, the staff of the post office with their six-star service flag and representatives of the Salvation Army, Odd Fellows, Woodmen and Elks. Students from all of Redlands' schools followed high school cadets. Aaron Leipsic decorated his automobile with flowers, with the word "peace" on the sides in large letters. Interestingly, several effigies of the Kaiser found their way into the

parade, including one in which the Kaiser was hanging by his heels from the top of the truck as individuals portrayed Satan and his assistants. Another featured Davis Donald carrying a coffin for the Kaiser on his trailer. In all, some 130 automobiles followed the marchers in the parades, each decorated patriotically for the occasion. Flags and bunting decorated every building downtown. As day turned into night, celebrations ended with a large bonfire across from city hall. At last, the war was over.

As peace dawned, the nation turned toward the future, with the words of Abraham Lincoln as true then as in 1865: "[L]et us strive on to finish the work we are in, to bind up the nation's wounds, to care for him who shall have borne the battle and for his widow and his orphan, to do all which may achieve and cherish a just and lasting peace among ourselves and with all nations."

2

DRAFTED INTO WAR

Once at war, America needed hundreds of thousands of men to aid in the global conflict, something a volunteer army could not provide. To fill the gap, a national army draft law was passed by Congress—the Selective Service Act—and signed by President Wilson on May 18, 1917. On June 5, 1917, a national registration of men aged twenty-one to thirty took place and included over nine and a half million men.

REGISTERING FOR WAR

Some concerns existed about how willing men would be to register for the draft, but Redlands men participated with little fuss. In the words of the *Facts* of June 6, 1917: "There was no disturbance. The men came quietly to the registration booths with the unostentatious enthusiasm of volunteers. The day was marked by a wonderful demonstration of quiet patriotism, the sort of patriotism that wins." The over 650 men who showed up in Redlands did not all come eager to volunteer, as many claimed exemptions on their cards, and the numerous non-citizens in the area could not be drafted.

Counties were split into draft exemption board districts, with Redlands in District 2 of San Bernardino County along with Mentone, Crafton, San Timoteo Canyon, Yucaipa, Highland, Loma Linda, Bryn Mawr, Colton,

Left: George Beattie, 1897.

Below: Redlands City Hall, 1933.

Patton and Grand Terrace. District 2's local exemption board included three men representing various communities in the district. George Beattie, chair, was an East Highland orange grower who would later write historical works about the area. The Redlands representative, and board secretary, was Arthur Grow, president of Redlands Abstract & Title Company. Walter Hebberd, Colton representative, was involved in the wholesale grocery business in Colton. These men served long and hard, sacrificing hours and days from their businesses from about June 1917 to the end of March 1919 and refusing any pay—although it was offered. Theirs was a hard job: determining the validity of draft exemption claims and classifying men. The office was in Redlands' city hall at Cajon Avenue and Vine Street. By at least June 1918, they had a hired clerk and stenographer, Ora R. Johnson, who also served until 1919. Johnson was only seventeen years old when she started work with the board.

Draft numbers were chosen by lottery in Washington, D.C., on July 20, 1917, and the list of men with their lottery drawing order was posted at city hall and published in newspapers. Each district in the country was assigned quotas of men based on their population. These men were to be sent to army training camps within the United States. By July 1917, District 2 had been told to provide 117 able-bodied men. Based on draft number order, sets of men were called for physicals at the local exemption board. Not knowing how many would actually appear, pass or be exempted, it was decided to call men from District 2 in several waves: on August 13 through 15, August 22 through 24 and September 10 through 12 in 1917.

PHYSICALS

Over 650 men were examined over the three time periods. Physicals included tests for vision, hearing, height, weight, lungs, heart, infectious diseases (such as tuberculosis and venereal disease), leg, arm, foot and hand conditions and mental state. If you were missing certain fingers or an eye or had flat feet you were exempted. Underlying these tests was the desire to draft men who were able to eat, follow instructions, walk or hike with heavy loads and pull a trigger on a weapon.

A *Facts* reporter provided an eyewitness account on August 13, 1917, of how the men of District 2 responded to their physicals at city hall:

PHYSICAL EXEMPTIONS 1917

(quotes from the War Department as noted in the Facts of July 26, 1917)

Mental: "Lack of normal understanding"

Skin: "Chronic, contagious and parasitic diseases, when severe and extensive: chronic ulcers, deep or extensive."

Head: "Abrupt depression in skull, the consequence of old fracture"

Spine: "Curvature, caries, abscess."

Ears: "All catarrhal and purulent forms of otitis media; perforation or tympanum"

Mouth: Draftees had to have four molars so they could chew food

Chest: "Diseases of lungs and heart, especially in flat or narrow or malformed chest...care must be taken not to ascribe to disease...the irregular action caused by the excessive use of tobacco."

Syphilis: No syphilis allowed.

Extremities: No chronic rheumatism; severe sprains; old dislocations that caused movement problems; "badly united fractures, caries, necrosis, atrophy or paralysis, extensive or adherent scars, permanent contraction of muscles."

Hands: "Webbed fingers, permanent flexion, extension or loss of motion of one or more fingers; loss or serious mutilation either thumb, total loss of index finger of the right hand, total loss of any two fingers of the same hand."

Lower extremities: "Pronounced varicose veins, especially when attended with edema or marks of ulceration, pronounced knuckles, club feet, flat feet, webbed toes, bunions, over-riding or marked displacement or deformity of any of the toes, hammer toes."

Height and weight: Accepted if approximately 118 pounds at five feet, one inch in height and up to 211 pounds if six feet, six inches in height.

As the first session of the board [physical exams] *opened at 8 o'clock this morning, anxious men, some smiling carelessly, others serious and sober-faced, crowded the corridors of the city hall awaiting their turn with the physicians. In the auditorium of the city hall rough temporary partitions have been constructed, forming dressing rooms on either side of the big hall. Across the front of the stage a large American flag was stretched, giving a certain amount of privacy to the men who were under the hands of the physicians.*

The work of examining was carried out with dispatch. The men were called in one or two at a time, given a slip for the examining physician to fill out and instructed to strip. Stark naked they stepped on to the scales, were weighed and their height taken. They were then turned over to the man who held their fate in his hands—the physician.

Rules for physical exams sent by War Department special order to local exemption boards included the following additional steps that examining physicians were to use:

The person under examination is required to leap directly up, to hop the length of the room on the ball of first one foot and then the other, to make a standing jump as far as possible and repeat it several times, to run the length of the room in double-time several times after which his heart and lungs are re-examined.

Of those examined from District 2, 151 failed their exam. Men could fail if their height to weight combination, based on charts, was off. John P. Tripp, partner in the Casa Loma Garage Company in Redlands, failed. The *Facts* report of August 15, 1917, stated, "He insisted on a reexamination but could not shorten his stature sufficiently to meet with his light weight. He was disappointed by a discharge." Henry Koenigheim, a manager and buyer for the Leipsic Department Store in Redlands, was also underweight but desired to be in the military. He was rejected both in his initial physical after the June 5, 1917 registration and when he tried to get into the aviation service. Later, on March 29, 1918, he was drafted to Camp Lewis, Washington, and proceeded on to Officers Training School, becoming a lieutenant by August 1918. Harold Fletcher, a British citizen working at Stutt Brothers Garage in Redlands, registered in June 1917. An alien, he still tried to enlist in the U.S. military but was denied due to being underweight. The Canadian army took him, and he left Redlands for Vancouver, British Columbia, on May 6, 1918.

Some men, despite poor vision, tried to get into the military. Herbert F. Wiese, a driver for John Alder of Redlands, was found to be blind in his right eye, failing his physical in September 1917. The military had organized a limited service category where some physical disabilities that kept men from full service still allowed them to enter the military in restricted capacities. Wiese was placed in this limited service category. On August 31, 1918, he was called for another physical prior to leaving on September 3 for Camp Bowie, Fort Worth, Texas. To his disgust, he again failed his physical due to his eyesight.

Alfred W. Winn, a salesman at Bennett's Bootery in Redlands, registered on June 5, 1917, with the registrar observing that his "left arm [was] burned, muscles stiff." He passed his physical in August 1917 and was finally drafted to Fort McDowell in May 1918, but there he was discharged due to the old burns, as noted in the *Facts* of June 1:

> *Al. W. Winn has returned from Camp McDowell, where he recently received an honorable discharge from the service because of injuries received in the explosion of an oil lamp about five years ago. Mr. Winn has made repeated attempts to get into the service. He is greatly disappointed over his failure to remain in the service, but his friends will realize the sincerity of his intentions.*

Alexander Echeverria was working as a laborer for East Highlands Orange Company in East Highlands, California, when he registered in June 1917. His two attempts to enlist were frustrated owing to an old fracture, a broken ankle from a baseball game while on the Redlands High School team. However, in August 1917, he passed his physical. Finally, he got himself drafted and sent to Camp Lewis on September 19, 1917.

Once past the initial physical in Redlands, the men were sent to Camp Lewis in Washington State. But they were not done with physicals. The army surgeons then reexamined everyone and released some who initially passed. Littleton Edmond Clinton, who had been working for the Redlands Sanitary Laundry, passed in Redlands but, once in camp, was discharged due to an ear problem. The government entrained him to Camp Kearny near San Diego, where he received his honorable discharge.

Dr. Charles L. Curtiss, a physician from Redlands working with draft physicals in Riverside County, presented a Redlands Fortnightly Club paper on May 23, 1918, during World War I. In it, he discussed causes of infection and disease in young men taking physicals for the draft. He particularly mentioned tuberculosis: "Tuberculosis in some part of the body, usually in the lungs, or a low grade chronic infection, somewhere else in the body, are the common causes of under weight." Three Redlands men were identified as tubercular on their June 1917 draft registration cards. One, Arthur C. Hartt, who was twenty-six years old, died by December 1917 or early January 1918.

Henry Wilson in front of his Union Oil Station, Citrus Avenue and Third Street, Redlands, about 1914.

While many men failed to pass the physical, there was the occasional enlistee who astonished everyone. Henry James Wilson, a self-employed oil merchant (his station appears to have been called by two names, either Redlands Oil Company or Union Oil Company), passed his physical exam in August 1917. He became known as the "perfect specimen," as quoted from the *Facts* of August 25, 1917:

> *Henry J. Wilson, passed yesterday by the physicians of the examining board, proved to be a perfect specimen of manhood. His examining physician brought him back to the board and said "Gentlemen, I wish to introduce to you a perfect specimen. He is A-1, one hundred per cent perfect. He ought to make a mighty good soldier." Wilson did not claim exemption. He will be one of those to go to a training camp in September.*

This "perfect specimen" was drafted and sent to Camp Lewis on October 3, 1917, where he became a corporal. His overseas duty began in July 1918, and by September 26, 1918, he was in the Meuse-Argonne Offensive in France. Although declared perfect for the army, by October 20, 1918, he wanted no more of war and was quoted in the *Facts*: "I have seen open warfare in all its phases, and it would suit me not to see any more.'" He arrived home in April 1919 as a sergeant. Wilson eventually became a commander of the Redlands American Legion Post 106 in 1933–34.

EXEMPTIONS

If you passed the physical, then you could claim an exemption that had to be proved. This would dramatically cut the pool of those eligible for camp. Out of the 652 men in District 2 who took physicals, 501 passed, the rest failing for physical reasons. But of those who passed, 367 claimed exemptions. Why and how did so many men from District 2 claim to be exempt from the draft even though they were physically fit?

Even before taking a physical, over two hundred men in the Redlands area were exempted, as they were non-citizens or "aliens." They had to prove their non-citizen status to be exempt. Aliens who registered in Redlands represented many countries of origin, including Canada, Cuba, Great Britain, Italy, Japan, Korea (under Japan at the time), Mexico, the Netherlands, Norway, the Philippines, the Portuguese Azores and Russia. Bunich Inouye, born in Hiroshima, Japan, and a Japanese citizen, was exempt from the draft. His registration card for June 5, 1917, showed he was a gardener for E.M. Lyon of Redlands. Santiago Garcia would have

EXEMPTED CATEGORIES IN 1917

Political office holders: executive, judicial, legislative
Ministers and theological students
Military personnel
Non-U.S. citizens (aliens)
Selected job-holders: such as postal service employees, federal armory, arsenal and navy yard workers
Pilots
Merchant marines
Those with financial dependents (such as a wife, children and/or parents)
Felons and the mentally unfit

been exempted on the basis of having a wife and six children to support on his track walker job for the Southern Pacific Railroad, but his Mexican citizenship was an even stronger exemption for him.

Some aliens insisted on being drafted. Robert B. Goodfellow, a citizen of Great Britain (Scotland), was an alien. He did not claim an alien exemption, passed the physical and was drafted. A *Facts* reporter noted on September 11, 1917, that "[w]hen asked if he wanted to go in the English army he said: 'No, I would rather not. I am an American now at heart, get my living here, and would rather fight with the Americans.'"

Karo Gegargian, an Armenian with Turkish citizenship (an alien), demanded to fight due to his hatred of Turkish killings of Armenians. Drafted on August 26, 1918, he failed to pass the physical at Camp Lewis due to ear problems. Undeterred, he returned to Redlands, and by November 4, as reported by the *Facts*, he still wanted to fight.

> *Karo Gargargian* [sic] *appeared before the local exemption board today a much distressed man. He brought with him a discharge from Camp Lewis, to which cantonment the board sent him about a month ago. Gargargian* [sic] *is an Armenian and several months ago he learned that the Turks were burying his people alive. He immediately came before the board and waived all claim for exemption and asked to be inducted into the service immediately. At Camp Lewis, however, he was found to have a defective ear and was sent home. The fact that Turkey is now out of the war and he cannot have his revenge directly does not quiet his ambition to get into the war and he insists he will find a place in some branch of the service.*

The bulk of the exemptions in Redlands occurred for men who had financial dependents. By law, if a man's wife was financially dependent on him and/or he had children, then he was exempt. In the Redlands area, over two hundred men who registered were married, and some already had up to five children. Charles Beal was married and had four children when he registered on June 5, 1917. Not only would he have been exempt due to his dependents, but he was also a U.S. Post Office employee.

If you had dependent parents or siblings, you also could be exempt. Clarence Mulder, born in Holland, had already taken out papers for citizenship, so he was eligible for the draft. A rancher for Harry H. Ford in the Redlands area, he was exempted since he was supporting his mother. Even though exempt, when he wanted to go fishing off San Pedro, he needed the District 2 Board to help him obtain a passport to prove his status.

Work in certain jobs exempted a few men in the Redlands area, mainly in the shipyards. Alvin Gray, a stonemason before the war, served with Redlands' Company G, Seventh California National Guard, for five months in 1916 at the Mexican border. By July 19, 1918, he was employed in the shipyards and exempt.

Leaving an exempt job changed a man's classification, usually to one making him more likely to be drafted. The public was asked in the *Facts* of August 27, 1918, to watch their exempt neighbors to see if they were lying or no longer had exempted jobs:

> *Herewith is published the names of all deferred classification men of district No. 2....The public is urged to look over this list, pick out the men they know and report to the board at Redlands names of men who are either not engaged in essential occupations or who have deferred classification without merit. This list does not include names of men whose cases have already been investigated.*

Some Redlands men claimed exemption for religious reasons, including Ashton Tatnall, a member of the Society of Friends, or Quakers. These men often were certified as non-combatants, drafted and sent to army camps, where

Warren James's World War I registration card (James grew up in Redlands).

they served in noncombat jobs. In September 1917, Tatnall was certified for noncombatant status but not drafted until April 26, 1918, to Camp Lewis. In September 1918, before the end of World War I, he received a furlough from military duty for one year to work in France and by early 1919 had joined the American Friends Reconstruction Unit in France, working to rebuild French villages. His name appears on the Redlands American Legion Post 106 World War I Veterans List, as he was in the army.

World War I exemption lapel pin.

Registered men were given a registration card to protect them from public retaliation if they were thought to be "slackers" or draft dodgers. If stopped by police or others, they could show the card to prove they had at least taken the first required step. But the government went further to protect those exempted. Each of these men received a dime-sized circular lapel pin with a U.S. shield and "Exempt" stamped on it. The District 2 exemption board received a box of these on August 31, 1917. The *Facts* of September 1, 1917, pointed out another problem about the exempt status: "Of course the board also provides each man with papers of discharge from the call in which he was examined so that 'slackers' will not get by if they have only an 'Exempt' button which they might have stolen from a man who was entitled to it."

OFF TO CAMP

On September 5, 1917, the first group of draftees from District 2 left for Camp Lewis, Washington, to prepare for the later, larger groups of men. Men with military service were most desirable. Three Redlands men qualified, including Rollo Holcomb, who co-owned the Triangle Candy

Panoramic view of Camp Lewis, Washington, September 1917. *Courtesy of the Library of Congress Prints and Photographs Division, Washington, D.C., Photo #pan.6a33881.*

Shop in Redlands with Frank J. Loge before the war and had three years of California National Guard experience.

Next, forty-seven draftees from District 2 entrained for Camp Lewis on September 19, 1917, twenty of them from Redlands. Redlands sent this group off to war with gusto. The Cope Commercial Company, across the tracks from the downtown Santa Fe Depot, was draped in large U.S. flags, and over one thousand people squeezed into the corridor area and tracks for the evening send-off at 11:00 p.m. The large group of new soldiers marched from city hall on Vine and Cajon Streets to the depot on Orange Street with the Redlands Municipal Band playing patriotic music, which they continued to do during the evening. A *Facts* reporter commented, "The departing soldiers were light-hearted and those final handshakes and embraces were cheery ones and were overflowing with confidence." Their youth (most in their twenties and with little or no military experience) and sense of adventure probably kept them from realizing what they were marching into. For the United States, it was early in World War I, with few deaths as yet. The American Civil War, ending over fifty years earlier, was two generations removed from most families' experience, and even the Spanish-American War was nearly twenty years in the past. Although a festive leave-taking, reality would catch up with this first large group of draftees from the Redlands area. Of the twenty Redlands men sent, five died: Harry Cook, Arthur Douglas, Teno Flores, Amzi Jeffers and Harry Lefler.

By October 3, another forty-seven men from District 2 left for Camp Lewis, including twenty from the Redlands area. On that evening, Redlanders came out to bid their men farewell. A *Facts* reporter captured the event in the October 4 publication:

Santa Fe Depot with Cope Commercial Company at right.

The enormous crowd with its laughing and cheering and the blaring of the band placed a bizarre tone upon the occasion and anything which might have given a plaintive or mournful note was swept away in the avalanche of cheerful farewells and the smiling, expectant faces of the departing men. The crowd at the station last night was fully as large as that which bade farewell to the second contingent from the district two weeks ago. The depot platform was packed with humanity and the mass of people surged clear out to the tracks. The special train of Pullmans arrived at 10:40 p.m. and departed at 10:55. The band was at the station and throughout the evening old familiar and patriotic selections were played. The first "chug, chug" of the departing train was echoed in the initial bar of the "Star Spangled Banner."

The Redlands Chamber of Commerce did not want the men to leave empty-handed, so during the day they asked merchants and citizens to donate candy, cigarettes and cigars. They outdid themselves. The *Facts* stated that the forty-seven men left with the following: "300 cigars, 250 packages of matches, 50 packages of gum, 50 packages of cigarettes, 48 cakes of chocolates, 10 pounds of candy and 48 tins of tobacco and cigarette papers."

Above: Redlands Chamber of Commerce, July 1913.

Left: Icle Buehler Pearson with her husband, Caleb Pearson, about April 1918. *Courtesy of Sharon Swan.*

This time, five men from Redlands would die in combat: Omer Buehler, Caleb Pearson, Charles Raisner, Ernest Richardson and Howard Thornton. A sixth, Harold Wright, died from an accident or other noncombat cause. A double tragedy occurred when Icle Buehler Pearson lost both her brother, Omer Buehler, and her husband, Caleb Pearson. She had married Caleb Pearson sometime after he registered for the draft on June 5, 1917.

On November 2, seventeen more men left, nine from Redlands, with one, Leonard Haws, later killed in action. The send-off was very similar to the previous ones, including decorations, the band and tobacco and candies given to the men.

AFRICAN AMERICAN DRAFTS

Nationwide, African American men—including those from Redlands—found that discrimination followed them throughout their military experience, including the draft process, training conditions and military occupations open to them. Even widows and mothers of African American men who died in service went on segregated government funded postwar trips (Gold Star Pilgrimages from 1930–33) to visit the graves of their family members in Europe, often on lesser-quality transportation.

On October 28, 1917, two men from Redlands were drafted and sent on a special train to Camp Lewis for "colored men." Robert Melvin Gault (farmer for Herbert L. Hubbard of Redlands) served in the 365th Infantry Regiment in France, one of the few African American groups that saw combat. On being interviewed by the *Facts* on April 12, 1919, he stated that he had fought on three fronts and "was in some warm fighting." Elwood E. Whiteside also left on this draft. He was accidently listed on several Redlands memorials in town as having died while serving in World War I, but it was actually another Redlands man, Roy Whiteside, who died while serving in the Canadian army.

While segregated, they still had a sendoff in Redlands, as noted in the *Facts* of October 29: "A large number of colored people of the city were at the station to wish them success and bid them goodbye. At Los Angeles the men boarded a special train which carried 100 colored men from Southern California to the cantonment."

Another small draft contingent was sent to Camp Lewis from Redlands on August 1, 1918, consisting exclusively of African Americans. Redlands men included David S. Goodwin (served in the 815th Pioneer Regiment) and Elmer H. Whiteside (brother of Elwood Whiteside). Goodwin was slated to go on the October 28, 1917 draft but was given a temporary agricultural exemption. (He also farmed for H.L. Hubbard of Redlands.)

PAUSE IN DRAFT TO RECLASSIFY

Due to the overwhelming number of men in U.S. military training camps, there was a pause in the larger drafts from November 2, 1917, to March 1918, with only small numbers of men called, usually for specialized jobs. Much to the shock of many men and their families, all old exemptions vanished on December 15, 1917. A new draft registration process was implemented that required men to claim and prove their exemptions before the physicals, reducing the number of required exams. A long questionnaire covered skills, exemption requests and other data that could be used to place men into five classes and allow the government to know of any special skills a man might have. The larger the classification number, the less likely a man was to be drafted. Mailing of questionnaires, their return and reclassification of the men took until February 1918. Physicals for District 2 men resumed on March 7 through 9, 1918, with one hundred Class 1 men being examined each day.

NEW DRAFT CLASSIFICATIONS

(selected examples given for each class)

Class 1: General service (physically fit); limited service (not eligible for all jobs); remediable defect

Class 2: Men with dependents not totally needing a man's financial support; necessary and skilled workers in agriculture and industry

Class 3: Men with dependent parent(s) and/or siblings; fire and policemen with at least three years of service; U.S. Post Office employees; armory or arsenal workers

Class 4: Men with wife and/or dependent children; mariners

Class 5: Office holders at federal or state level; ministers; military personnel; aliens; physically unfit; mentally unfit; morally unfit; pilots

By February 1918, standards for foot and dental problems were eased. The minimum accepted height moved from five feet, one inch down to four feet, ten inches. As reported by the *Facts*, if a man was overweight according to height-to-weight charts, it was allowable "unless the obesity interferes with normal physical activity."

Men with remediable physical defects could also be placed in Class 1 and drafted once their defect was fixed. For some men, this probably gave them a chance for a better life if they survived the war. Carl C. Baker's June 5, 1917 draft card claimed he had a "rupture and injured leg." This may have been the disability that placed him in the limited service category after his March 1918 physical. Baker had an operation before May 20, 1918, that addressed his problems and changed him out of the limited service category. He was drafted and sent to Camp Kearny on June 24, 1918, and eventually went overseas.

RESTART OF DRAFT CALLS

Over the next few months, a series of smaller draft groups left Redlands, starting on March 29, 1918. Most went to Camp Lewis and were usually given town sendoffs. Perhaps due to less restrictive physical exams or better health, men previously turned down were now being drafted. By May 1918, District 2 draftees scattered to other camps besides Camp Lewis. Fort McDowell on Angel Island in San Francisco had received six Redlands men by May 1, 1918. Of these, William Doell, Walter Inman and Carl Olson found themselves serving in Siberia by October 1918. Carl Olson landed at Vladivostok, went inland to fight communists and experienced temperatures as low as 59 below zero.

A second draft registration of men who turned twenty-one after June 5, 1917, was held on June 5, 1918, to obtain more men for the army. Twenty-seven of the men were from Redlands. Physicals occurred on July 28, and the first men from this group were finally drafted by early September 1918.

Summer 1918 continued the series of smaller drafts; on June 24, thirty-two men from District 2 left for Camp Kearny in the San Diego area. Some of these men served overseas in the 144th Field Artillery (known as the California Grizzlies). One, Albert Smith, a printer with the *Redlands Daily Review* before the war, was drafted on June 24, 1918, to Camp Kearny and ended up in the Grizzlies. Although not in combat, he contracted the flu and

Panoramic view of Camp Kearny near San Diego, California, about 1918. *Courtesy of the Library of Congress Prints and Photographs Division, Washington, D.C., photo #pan.6a30548.*

Artillery and trench warfare practice, Camp Kearny, World War I. *Courtesy of the American Unofficial Collection of World War I Photos, photo #26434001, RG 165, National Archives and Records Administration.*

had an eye complication that put him in the hospital for a short time before his release.

As the summer of 1918 progressed, draftees were reclassified so that more men could be sent to war. Some reclassifications came from physical exam results. Now if you had lost your left thumb or one finger on either hand, except the right index one, you could qualify for general service (Class 1). The right thumb and index finger would be needed for firing a gun.

Deafness in one ear or blindness in one eye or loss of the right thumb would still qualify you for limited service. Past physical results had to be reexamined to see if men could be reclassified.

Many other reclassifications came from a group who married after May 18, 1917, the day President Wilson signed the Selective Service Act. This was viewed by many people as cheating to avoid the draft. Due to a lack of draftable men, the board could not continue to exclude those who had clearly married after the law was signed. Herbert S. Nicks, clerk at the Standard Oil Company of Redlands, married after May 18, 1917. By July 1918, he was viewed as eligible for the draft and transferred from Class 4 to Class 1 and sent off to camp. Alfred T. Parker got caught in the drafting of married men but with a twist. Married at the time of the first draft registration, he had divorced by June 1917 and then remarried in December 1917. By March 1918, the need for Class 1 men was getting desperate, and since he remarried after the war started, he was now assigned to that class and drafted on August 6, 1918.

INFLUENZA IN THE MILITARY CAMPS

James Backus and Al Winn, both limited service men, were drafted on September 3, 1918, to Camp Bowie, near Fort Worth, Texas. Winn's early story has already been told; he had been burned in an oil lamp explosion and disqualified twice. Backus's and Winn's draft stories illustrate the effect of the influenza epidemic of fall 1918 on military camps.

Backus was among those who registered on June 5, 1917, but his physical exam in September listed him as physically deficient, which at that time meant he was exempt from the draft. However, on December 15, 1917, draft regulations changed, canceling all previous exemptions. Backus was called on March 7, 1918, for his next physical. Originally deemed physically deficient for service, the doctors found his physical condition unclear enough that he was told to report to the medical advisory board in San Bernardino, where a team of specialized physicians checked men in this category. On April 4, 1918, the decision came back: he was qualified for limited service. Winn went as an alternate replacing Herbert Wiese, the man mentioned earlier who failed his physical due to poor eyesight.

Backus and Winn left Redlands on the evening of September 3, 1918, by train, planning a through trip to the Fort Worth area. However, at Barstow they paused with enough time to discover that a special troop train from

San Francisco was coming through and, wanting to join that train, swapped their tickets. They arrived at Fort Worth on September 6 with a trainload of soldiers from San Francisco, plus those who boarded in Southern California, Arizona, New Mexico and Texas. They were marched to the camp with a band leading them on their way.

Newly arrived recruits were not immediately allowed to mix with the main group of soldiers at the camp until declared disease free. Winn's letter of September 9 described the "detention camp" where he and Backus first lived:

> *I am in detention camp now for fourteen days, which we new rookies term being in prison, and it is termed just right. It is a camp fenced off with heavy barbed wire, with guards walking past outside day and night. After the fourteen days are up, if some disease has not broken out in detention camp, we will then be transferred to the regular camp, where we will have some privileges. Jim Backus is in the tent with me with four other boys from California, San Diego and San Francisco.*

The army used Camp Bowie, situated on the western outskirts of Fort Worth, Texas, as a training site for the infantry. On September 9, while in detention, Backus wrote a letter to the Redlands exemption board stating, "I am glad to get in and I have a good place here and good officers." Interestingly, both Winn and Backus apparently were declared fit for general service, not limited service, in a note to the District 2 exemption board dated October 1, 1918.

The idea of a quarantine sounded good and probably worked in many cases. But the horrendous influenza epidemic of 1918–19 had already started in many military camps around the country and would soon engulf Camp Bowie. The flu hit the camp hard by mid-October 1918, with men streaming into the base hospital and many dying from complications due to pneumonia. Barely out of the detention camp and into training, Backus fell ill with the flu. He was under a doctor's care starting on October 12. Backus's youngest sister, Florence, lived in Redlands, and it was she who received the alarming message on October 14 that her brother was very ill with the flu at Camp Bowie. According to the *Facts* of October 14, Camp Bowie "is at present quarantined on account of Spanish influenza." Florence then received the tragic news of her only brother's death on October 20—the same day he died of pneumonia at the Camp Bowie base hospital. Adding to her problems, Florence herself had the flu and was sent to her maternal aunt's home in Riverside that same day due to her condition.

James Backus grave marker, Hillside Memorial Park, Redlands, California. *Courtesy of Ann Deegan.*

Winn, the man who less than two months earlier took the adventurous train ride to Camp Bowie with Backus and who had been his tent mate now had the sad duty of accompanying Backus's body back to Redlands for burial. The funeral at Cortner Bros. and burial at Hillside Memorial Park occurred on October 25, the day his body arrived in Redlands. Winn was also one of the pallbearers at the funeral service. James Backus gave his life for his country, no matter the length of military service or cause of death.

The deadly influenza pandemic interfered with the work of sending men to camp for training. From early September through much of October 1918, military camps within the U.S. struggled with hundreds of flu deaths and the seemingly uncontrollable spread of the disease. Yet another drafted Redlands man, Jesse Wheaton, called up on July 22, 1918, died of the flu. He died on October 21, 1918, at Camp Lewis, Washington. In late September, the provost marshal canceled the next two draft calls to camps.

RUNNING OUT OF MEN

The September 5, 1918 draft of seventeen men to Camp Kearny, California, included some of the last Class 1 Redlands men from the large June 5, 1917 registration but saw the first addition of Redlands men from the June 5, 1918 one. It took three months to get the first of the Redlands men from the June 5, 1918 registration into the service. A supplemental registration on August 24, 1918, was designed to record those few men who turned twenty-one between June 6, 1918, and August 24, 1918. Only six men appeared from Redlands. Classification and physicals for these men went swiftly, and by October 23—two months after registering—the first men from that group were drafted.

By late summer 1918, the ready pool of qualified registered men aged twenty-one to thirty was rapidly disappearing. An early October 1918 draft call would take almost all the rest of the June and August 1918 registered men. The provost marshal did not want to dip into the classes of deferred men until the age range for the draft was widened. This large registration was to include all men from eighteen to forty-five years of age, drafting first those nineteen through thirty-six.

A *Facts* article of August 14, 1918, toyed with the idea of who would disappear from Redlands in the older age range if men were called to age forty-five. Men such as city engineer George S. Hinckley, superintendent of schools Henry Clement and chamber of commerce secretary A.E. Isham would have been in that age range. Another man, not noted in that article, was Arthur Grow, secretary of the District 2 Exemption Board, who completed a draft card, as he was forty-three years old.

District 2 was going to need clerical help to process the anticipated massive September 12, 1918 registration paperwork. A limited service draft about September 11, 1918, sent three Redlands men off to Presidio, San Francisco, to prepare for this work. Harvey Dodson and Volney Kincaid were promptly sent back to the Redlands Exemption Board by September 22. Kincaid had been working at the First National Bank of Redlands prior to his service, while Harvey Dodson was bookkeeper for Gold Buckle Association in East Highland. Lyle Doan was sent to San Bernardino as a clerk for the medical advisory board that served District 2 as well as other districts. He had been a dry goods salesman with C.W. Merriman Dry Goods of Redlands. These men worked about four months and then were discharged from the army.

For Redlands, over 760 men completed a draft registration card on September 12, 1918. After classifying the men aged nineteen to thirty-six, those Class 1 from District 2 were called for physicals on November 7 and 8.

As the flu epidemic eased up, the drafts began again. By October 23, District 2 was called to send fifteen men to Fort Rosecrans, San Diego, for heavy artillery training. By now, few eligible men remained from any of the earlier registrations, and the men of the September 12 registration were not yet processed through for the draft. Seven men from Redlands were to leave, including four from the June 5, 1917 registration, one from June 5, 1918, and two from the August 24 registration. The flu epidemic still affected this group, as the last physicals done the afternoon before leaving found Mark Higgins, employed by Marigold Farms in Redlands in June 1918, too ill to go. He was replaced with an alternate. The draft board did not give up on him, though, drafting him on November 11.

Higgins's alternate, Roy Choi, was an alien, born in Korea. When he registered on June 5, 1917, he declared his prior military experience as three years in the Korean army. Now at age thirty-one, he showed a desire to serve in the U.S. Army, even though he was not a citizen. Selected for an August 26, 1918 draft to Camp Lewis, the local board balked and said no, as another Korean man had not been accepted at Camp Lewis earlier. He finally got in as an alternate on this draft of October 23.

Daniel Kane, another alien (citizen of Great Britain), also got into the U.S. Army through this draft. On May 9, 1918, the U.S. naturalization law was changed to ease the process for current non-citizen military personnel and veterans to become U.S. citizens. Kane received his naturalization papers on November 20, 1918, while still in the army at Fort Rosecrans.

November 1918 produced one of the most bizarre draft stories from Redlands. The largest draft contingent yet to come from District 2 included sixty-six men (thirty-five from Redlands) due to leave November 11. Redlands men were taken from the June 5, 1917 (four), June 5, 1918 (one) and August 24, 1918 (two) registrations and for the first time from the September 12, 1918 registration (twenty-eight). Also, the first group of men between nineteen and twenty-one years old were drafted (nineteen from Redlands) while eight men ages thirty-three to thirty-six years old were called from Redlands. Men for this draft quit such jobs as musician, gardener, rancher, box maker, carpenter, theater manager and mechanic. War was no longer a great adventure, as they had heard of the deaths of friends and family and wounding of others. The men from the September 12 registration had just a few days earlier, on November 7 and 8, had their physicals that decided their fate.

At 4:00 p.m. on November 10, the men were inducted into the army, and at 5:30 p.m., they attended a banquet given at the Suess Cafeteria. Inspirational speakers told them about the evils of drinking, the mayor spoke of the pride of Redlands that they would serve and yet another speaker stressed how healthy the military made young men, finishing with a talk about taking advantage of the opportunities that they would have. These men were then allowed to return to their homes for the night. All arrived at 8:00 a.m. on November 11 for yet another physical before entraining for Fort Kelly, Texas. One man failed due to flu-like symptoms, hopefully not infecting others. They then boarded the Pacific Electric car waiting to leave at 9:10 a.m.

Today, we know that November 11, 1918, marked the armistice, or ceasefire, with the Germans. At 11:00 a.m. in Europe, the fighting stopped. The *Facts* of November 11 stated that celebrating in Redlands started very early in the morning of that day. But the men waiting on the train could still be sent to camp, and a ceasefire was not a peace treaty; tensions would have been high. As the minutes ticked down for departure, a telegram arrived at 9:00 a.m. stating that all trains due to leave to military camps with drafted men were to stop and return to their points of origin. By just ten minutes, these sixty-six men had missed the draft. The rejoicing among the men and their families and friends must have been staggering.

POSTWAR EXEMPTION BOARD WORK

The war had ended, but the District 2 exemption board kept busy compiling reports and retrieving all of its draft records. By March 31, 1919, it had finally finished the work and sent eighteen cases of records to Washington, D.C. From the time of the board's inception in June 1917 until it disbanded, Beattie, Grow and Hebberd worked on the board. Based on the board's records, over six hundred men were drafted into the army through District 2 (not just Redlands). All the men's names and questionnaires were part of the records sent away to be stored in War Department vaults. As a *Facts* reporter stated on March 27, 1919, "These records, which are most complete in every respect, will probably be consulted by people centuries later, by those wishing to learn family history." Truly foretelling the future, the reporter was correct; these records from World War I have been consulted today to write this book, including the draft cards filled out so long ago.

3

CHOOSING TO SERVE

ENLISTING

Men from the Redlands area enlisted from shortly before World War I until the end of the war on November 11, 1918. Draftees could not be younger than twenty-one or older than thirty until September 1918, when men nineteen to thirty-six years old became eligible. Enlistees could be as young as eighteen or as old as forty. Some men younger than eighteen also managed to enlist. The marines and navy never were part of the draft.

At least 450 Redlands men enlisted, probably many more. Because of the variety of occupations and the scattered enlistments (some one man at a time), this chapter will focus on several of the largest groups of enlistees from Redlands and highlight a few others.

COMPANY G, SEVENTH CALIFORNIA REGIMENT, NATIONAL GUARD

Redlands' own Company G of the California National Guard formed in 1892. Called up for the Spanish-American War in 1898, it only got as far as San Francisco. From June to November 1916, the company served on the Arizona border with Mexico as part of the defense against Pancho Villa's raids. Men joined from Redlands but also from surrounding communities such as Bryn Mawr and Banning.

Company G was summoned to camp in Arcadia, California, once Congress voted for war on April 4, 1917. The *Facts* reported on April 4:

> *Hundreds of people awaited the company at the point of Departure* [in Redlands]. *Hundreds of people cheered and applauded as strains of martial music heralded their approach from the armory. There was a thrill of pride that lit up every face in the crowd as the boys marched up Orange street and stood at attention before the speakers' stand at the Triangle. And as they stood there with "Old Glory" floating above them from the flagstaff the full significance of the great events that have crowded the last week came sharply home to everyone. Redlands was giving her boys to defend the flag and the country it stands for....* [T]*he band struck up "The Girl I Left Behind Me," and the boys filed into the big Pacific Electric car which was waiting to bear them to the mobilization point at Arcadia. The people crowded about the car to utilize to the utmost the few moments before the company pulled out. As the car passed slowly down Orange street the crowd followed, shouting their last farewells.*

And so Company G, sixty-six strong, went off to war. From Arcadia, California, they went to North Island, San Diego, for guard duty and then on to what would become the enormous training facility at Camp Kearny near San Diego. Months passed after their eager farewell to join the fighting, yet the men remained at Camp Kearny. They lost Private Edgar Putnam on October 7. His is the story of the first Redlands man to die in service during World War I.

Edgar Fay Putnam, born in 1898 in Nebraska, came with his family of three brothers and two sisters, plus aunts, uncles and grandparents, to Redlands around 1902. Starting in 1909, his father, Willis Putnam, and then two elder brothers, Harold and Clyde, owned and ran the University Grocery on Stillman Avenue near the University of Redlands. His father also served on the Redlands public school board from at least 1912 to 1918.

Putnam, aged eighteen when World War I started in April 1917, could not yet be drafted, as he was under twenty-one. But he could enlist and quit in his senior year of high school before April 4 to join Company G. By April 8, Private Putnam had done so.

Back home, his Redlands High School class was planning its graduation for June 12. The U.S. Army and Redlands High School allowed Putnam and three of his Company G fellow soldiers to return in uniform and graduate despite missing over two months of their senior years. John Allen,

Above: Putnam family University Grocery Store, 1909, Edgar Putnam at far right.

Right: Edgar Putnam, World War I. *Courtesy of the Putnam family.*

Robert Burke, Clyde Cook and Putnam attended the ceremony to receive their diplomas.

As far as is known, a healthy Putnam participated in Company G work. While at Camp Kearny, he was allowed leave on Sunday, October 7, 1917, to visit a friend's home in San Diego. He became ill there that evening and died. Putnam's sudden death shocked family and friends. On receipt of the news in Redlands on October 8, 1917, the *Facts* published an article about his death:

> *The news came as a severe shock to relatives here, as no intimation had been received other than decedent [Edgar Putnam] was enjoying his usual good health. Captain Ernest Danielson, commanding officer of Co. G, to which company Putnam belonged, is in Redlands today [October 8, 1917] on furlough. When informed he was considerably surprised and grieved. He stated that when last he saw decedent he was in the best of health.*

The military conducted an autopsy and had an inquest on October 8 to determine why this apparently healthy man suddenly died. Medical data indicated that he died from problems related to a dilated heart.

Notified by telegram on October 8, his family organized his funeral service for Thursday, October 11 at the First Methodist Church of Redlands. The transit permit for Putnam's body, allowing transport from San Diego to Redlands, revealed that one of his fellow Redlands High School graduates from the class of 1917, Second Lieutenant Clyde Cook, was called on to give personal data about Putnam. This was surely a difficult task for this officer.

A large crowd gathered at the church, including Redlands High School students and members of Company G from San Diego. Six of the pallbearers were from Company G, a fitting tribute to this young man. They included Captain Ernest L. Danielson, Corporal Claude H. McMillan, Paul A. Lockwood, Henry E. Taylor, Frank L. Zimmerman and the Company G bugler, Herbert Hill. Words from the *Facts* of October 11, 1917, give some insight into his character:

> *All who were acquainted with Edgar Putnam have nothing but the highest praise for his personality and patriotism. He had innumerable friends because of his excellent traits of character and those who knew him can hardly realize he is gone; he was too much alive, too vivid a personality. Because his capacity for generosity seemed so spontaneous his friends now*

realize that they accepted it all too much as a matter of course. He is dead, but his work and the example he has set live after him.

The graveside service in Hillside Memorial Park of Redlands included the playing of "Taps" and a firing squad provided by Company K of San Bernardino, another California National Guard unit. It must have been a very sad and solemn occasion, the first military service death in Redlands and for a man of such a young age. Just a few months earlier, he had been at his Redlands High School graduation looking forward to life. Willing and eager to serve, he gave his life. Whether he died in battle or not, he was a fatality of war.

As the war progressed, military units were reshuffled and renamed, a fate that would fall on Company G. By late September 1917, the 7th Regiment of the California National Guard became part of the 160th Infantry Regiment. Then the ultimate blow fell in mid-October, when Redlands' own Company G ceased to exist, as it was merged into Company C of the 160th Infantry Regiment.

Company C finally left Camp Kearny in late July or early August 1918, over a year after the men left Redlands. Part of their role was to supply men to other units. Lieutenant Paul D. Smith entered Company G as a sergeant, was sent to officers' training camp and as a new lieutenant went to a different unit, the 361st Infantry Regiment in the 91st Division. He was killed in the Meuse-Argonne Offensive probably on September 26, 1918. Private Manuel Marquez left the original Company G earlier in the war and was sent to France. He was with the 104th Infantry Regiment, 26th Division, when he was killed in action on October 17, 1918, also probably during the Meuse-Argonne fighting.

The excitement must have built as word was received back in Redlands of the landing on the East Coast of wave after wave of military men returning after the war's end. On April 7, 1919, the *Facts* headline stated "Local Soldiers Coming April 12" and "Word Received that Former Seventh Regiment Boys Are En Route." The former Company G men crossed the country by train to Los Angeles and on to Camp Kearny, where they were given their discharges. Many served from April 4, 1917, into 1919.

CALIFORNIA GRIZZLIES

144th California Field Artillery Regiment

Other Redlands men also enlisted as a group to fight in the war. The California Grizzlies, a field artillery regiment, began recruiting volunteers in California around July 1917. The Grizzlies received its name from being an all-volunteer regiment made up of men from California. As mentioned in the *Facts* of October 27, 1917, "The unit is distinctly Californian and the only volunteer regiment in the army organized since the war started."

On August 11, 1917, twelve Redlands men left to join the Grizzlies. Friends and family gathered to see them off to Camp Tanforan in San Bruno, California, for their first training. Only one other group of soldiers, Company G, had as yet left from Redlands to go to war. By fall 1917, waves of draftees would follow.

By late October 1917, the Grizzlies changed from a light to a heavy artillery regiment, requiring an influx of another four hundred men. Sometime in late October or early November, the regiment moved to Camp Kearny for further training. This was a desirable organization but now in need of vigorous recruiting. Words from a *Facts* reporter on October 25, 1917, give some insight into what might have attracted men to join this group:

> *Emphasis is being laid on the securing of men of the highest character and ability. From every walk of life they have come and it has developed that "The Grizzlies" are composed of specialists of every variety, there are cowboys, polo players, capitalists, ranchers, mechanics, merchants clerks, stenographers, chauffeurs, electricians, blacksmiths, telegraphers, lawyers, engineers, artists, newspapermen and ex-soldiers. A very high percentage of the men are college graduates or former college men.*

The twenty-five Redlands-area men who joined included at least eighteen high school graduates, twelve from Redlands High School and six from other schools. The nine college graduates or students in college included two University of Redlands graduates and six more attending, plus one man, Stanley Morrison, who was at Harvard Law School in June 1917. This was truly an impressive group of recruits in terms of education for this time period.

Camp amenities included athletics. One recruiter stated on November 2, 1917, in the *Facts* that "all forms of athletic activity are provided for the men

Stanley Morrison, World War I. *Courtesy of Anne Ouelette.*

at camp. One hour a day is devoted to various sports and football, baseball, golf, tennis and polo teams have been organized." Some of the Redlands men were fine athletes before entering the service, including Oliver Weed (Redlands High School graduate in 1914 and University of Redlands student). Weed was an outstanding football player at the University of Redlands in the fall of 1916. He continued his football playing while at Camp Kearny, where rival teams staged competitions. Unfortunately, by the time Weed returned to Redlands in July 1919, he was diagnosed with a broken foot, which put him in the hospital for a while. As stated in the *Facts* of July 23, 1919:

> *It is expected that Weed will return to the University of Redlands in the fall* [1919] *to complete his course and he was counted upon heavily for the football team, having distinguished himself in the service football teams. His injury may prevent his playing and in that event will be a great disappointment to Weed and his friends.*

Names would appear in the newspaper of local men who supposedly had "signed up" or "enlisted" in the Grizzlies only to find that they failed the physical or for some other reason were not accepted into the unit. By July 1917, men who were given an exemption from the draft due to dependents (such as an elderly mother) could sit out the war. Carl Olson, a deliveryman for the Model Creamery in Redlands, claimed that he needed to be exempt to care for his dependent parents. The government granted him the exemption at least by August 1917. However, in November 1917, he must have changed his mind and tried to enlist in the Grizzlies. He quit his job, had at least one going away party and received a wristwatch from his friends, who also went to the train station to see him off. Dramatically, a telegram arrived stating that those men with dependents would not be allowed to enlist, including Carl Olson. His was not the only example of denial to enlist due to dependents. However, as the war continued into the spring of 1918, the pool of draftable U.S. men was shrinking. Rules began to change to ease physical exam restrictions, and some reclassifying of men occurred—including to those with dependents. Carl Olson fell into the latter category and was drafted on May 1, 1918. He was eventually sent to the Siberian front, where he fought.

The Grizzlies continued to train at Camp Kearny at least until April 1918. During that time, one Redlands man, Willard Best, was lost due to an accident. War conjures up deaths in combat or serious wounds but not from a lethal diving accident.

Redlands High School students who died in World War I from the 1919 *Makio*. *From left to right* are (*bottom row*) William Carson, George Corwin and Edgar Putnam; (*middle row*) Willard Best, Dean Nethaway and Paul Sawyer; (*top row*) Silas Ballard, Ben Berry and Joseph Pray.

Willard R. Best was born in Oak Glen, California, in December 1896 to Fred and Eva Best into a family who would eventually provide him with three brothers and one sister. At three years of age, he was living in Redlands. The family moved to Texas but returned to Redlands at least by 1914, and Best attended Redlands High School. Eventually, he graduated from Beaumont High. It was Best's years in Redlands and attendance at its high school that later caused the town to claim him as one of their own.

Best enlisted in the Grizzlies in November 1917 at just short of twenty-one years of age and joined the unit at Camp Kearny. Still at Camp Kearny by April 1918, Willard had become a private first class with the Headquarters Company. A *Facts* reporter related on April 17, 1918, that Best "stood remarkably high in his company, both as regards his military duties and his general deportment. He was universally liked and respected."

On April 5, 1918, at a distance of about seven miles from Camp Kearny, Best and other soldiers were on a hike. Whether anyone else went in swimming is unknown, but he dove off an embankment into a stream not realizing that the water was extremely shallow. The result was a broken neck. Best survived the initial broken neck and was rushed back to the Base Hospital at Camp Kearny. There it was determined that he had broken his neck at the sixth cervical vertebra and had crushed and lacerated his spinal cord at that same point, a serious, paralyzing injury. The medical certificate stated he dove off a six-foot bank into six inches of water. The trauma of the event and efforts to get him back to camp were devastating, both to him and his fellow young soldiers. Despite all efforts, he died on April 15 after lingering for ten days.

Within three days, on April 18, 1918, at 10:00 a.m., the funeral of Best was taking place in Redlands. Services were at the Dow and Fitzsimmons Chapel. The Reverend George H. Wixom, San Bernardino pastor of the Reorganized Church of Jesus Christ of Latter-day Saints in San Bernardino, performed the service. Best's military company sent flowers. Interment was in Hillside Memorial Park, Redlands. At this time, only two other men from the Redlands area had died in World War I service, neither of them from combat. (Edgar Putnam died on October 7, 1917, and Alan Bedell died on February 24, 1918.)

Best's death was shocking and tragic. At least we know something of the man and the respect he drew from his short life. Although he did not die in combat, he was still honored by his community for service in wartime.

The men of the Grizzlies finally sailed from the East Coast to Liverpool, England, in late August or early September 1918 and proceeded on to

Bordeaux, France. They moved to a small village near Clermont-Ferrand, France, where a large artillery range was available for the six-inch guns they were to use. They never got into combat, as their goal of a November 16, 1918 entry ended with the November 11 ceasefire. Compared to many military units, the Grizzlies had a very rapid exit from France, getting back to Bordeaux in late December 1918 and across the Atlantic to Camp Merritt, New Jersey. Then a cross-country train ride landed them back in Redlands in late January 1919.

FELLED BY INFLUENZA

The influenza pandemic started its appearance in the summer of 1918 and exploded in U.S. military camps and overseas in September and October 1918, resulting in thousands of deaths. This flu was particularly lethal if it progressed into pneumonia and hit hard among the young military men.

From September through November 1918, eight Redlands-area men in military service and one woman died in the influenza pandemic. One additional man died from the disease in January 1919. These deaths took place in camps across the United States, in an army hospital in the Bronx and one at sea. All apparently got the flu that developed into lethal pneumonia. Leland Rausch, a machinist's mate first class on a submarine in the navy, died on September 29 in Philadelphia. He had been in the navy since July 12, 1918, and made a trip on the small H-2 submarine from San Pedro, California, through the Panama Canal up to the East Coast in October 1917. Michael Jennings died at sea on October 5. His story is told within this chapter. Dean Nethaway died on October 7 in Camp Logan, Houston, Texas (see page 71). A USC law graduate, he was a sergeant in the army in an ordnance group. George Corwin died at Camp Morrison near Newport News, Virginia, just one day later (see page 71). A member of the Thirty-Sixth Balloon Company of the army, he had been issued equipment for overseas just before he died. Because the flu epidemic had hit Redlands, his funeral was restricted to his mother's home in Highland rather than at a more public gathering place. The one woman from the Redlands area who died in service was Maybelle Wellman, a nurse serving with the army in the Bronx, New York. She died on October 15 from the flu. A limited service man, James Backus, died on October 20. Jesse Wheaton died on October 21 at Camp Lewis, where he served with an army field artillery unit, a draftee

USS H-2 submarine No. 29 in January 1914 off Mare Island, California. *Courtesy of the Naval History and Heritage Command, photo #NH45619.*

Banford Long permit for removal and burial, October 27, 1918.

from July 22, 1918. Banford Long died at Fort Benjamin Harrison, Indiana, around October 25. He had worked as a railroad fireman shoveling coal for the Santa Fe Railroad before the war and apparently was drafted to this fort, where railroad men trained. Paul Sawyer died on November 24, after the war had ended (see page 71). He, too, was a machinist's mate first class in the submarine section of the navy and died at the Submarine Base Hospital in San Pedro, California. One more man, Robert Owen, died in January 1919 of the flu at Vancouver Barracks, Washington.

The story of Michael Stanley Jennings, an army enlistee who died of the flu, is used as an example of the effect the flu had on troops and tells the story of the 319th Engineers recruited from the far western states.

Born in Florida in 1890, Jennings knew the Mission, Loma Linda and Bryn Mawr farming areas west of Redlands from about 1900. He worked as a butcher in 1910, perhaps in his father's meat market in Redlands. His father's orange grove in the Mission area provided him with employment by 1917.

Jennings registered for the World War I draft on June 5, 1917, but failed his physical in September, exempting him from military service. The repeal of all draft exemptions on December 15, 1917, meant another physical for Jennings, this one on March 7, 1918. This time, he passed, making him draft eligible. But Jennings, like many faced with the draft, did not want the army to decide what he would do; instead, he opted to enlist in the 319th Engineers of the 8th Army Division. His brother, Joseph, also joined the 319th Engineers. Stanley and Joseph Jennings left by train for Camp Fremont near Palo Alto on March 12, 1918, just five days after Stanley passed his army physical. Joseph apparently did not remain with the 319th and reached the European theater of war around May 1918 while Stanley was still at Camp Fremont.

The 319th Engineers obtained men mainly from California, Oregon, Washington, Idaho and Nevada. Recruiters for this group appeared in Redlands at least by March 8, 1918. Nine men from Redlands joined. The group consisted of an electrician (Robert B. Goodfellow), a plumber with the Redlands City Water Department (Kenneth C. Johnson), two farm workers (the two Jennings brothers), two laborers (John Curtis and Cyrus Waters), a University of Redlands student (Edwin Bamford), an insurance agent for Metropolitan Life Insurance Company (John Nicks) and one man of unknown occupation (Roy Browning).

After joining in March 1918 and training for several months, Jennings and the 319th Engineers were nearing their time to be shipped overseas to France. Unfortunately, their September 1918 travel time occurred as a particularly deadly influenza was sweeping the world. Crowded conditions in military camps, in both the United States and Europe; on troop transport ships; and in the trenches of France helped to increase the severity and spread the transmission of influenza in the summer and fall of 1918. Personnel in the Office of the Surgeon General of the U.S. Army recognized the high morbidity and mortality on the troop ships and asked for less crowding on board and one week quarantine of soldiers before getting on ships. (This flu often had a twenty-four- to forty-eight-hour incubation period before symptoms appeared.) The request was denied because it would delay moving men overseas. In France, the Meuse-Argonne Offensive was starting, and General Peyton C. March, chief of staff of the army, stated, "If American divisions stopped arriving in France, whatever the reason, German morale might soar." The Surgeon General's Office took the request all the way to President Wilson but was refused.

Instead of temporarily stopping these ships or drastically decreasing their troop capacity, men were checked for the flu before boarding. If you were sick, you stayed in the United States. But this flu, with its twenty-four- to forty-eight-hour incubation period, was just right for apparently well soldiers to get on board, become sick and pass the flu along in tight quarters.

An example of flu on board troop transports was found on a huge German passenger liner captured at a U.S. port at the war's outbreak and renamed the *Leviathan*. One of its voyages to Europe in late September–early October 1918 revealed the results of rampant flu on board as described by Lyman King, editor of the *Redlands Daily Facts*, who served with the Young Men's Christian Association in France and observed the ship's arrival in Brest (published in the *Facts* on November 18, 1918):

> *The writer has seen no statement of the large number of deaths caused by influenza and pneumonia on the transports en route to Europe from America during the month of October* [1918]. *With the war over* [November 11, 1918] *there is no reason now that this should not be told. Thousands of precious lives have been given to their country through this one agency of destruction. I was in Brest in the early days of October* [1918]. *Brest is the port at which the American transports landed their men. The convoy which came while I was there had more than 500 dead on the several ships which composed it. The* Leviathan *(the old* Vaterland*) had 87 corpses when it dropped anchor in the harbor. Another vessel had 62. These figures are authentic. They came from men who were in a position to know. And this convoy, in addition to 500 men who had died en route, turned approximately 2000 cases of pneumonia into the general hospital at Brest.*

SS *Leviathan*, troop transport, returning to the United States, March 1919. *Courtesy of the American Unofficial Collection of World War I Photos, RG 165, National Archives and Records Administration, photo #26433817.*

The *Leviathan* and other ships would continue to move about 100,000 troops from the United States to Europe from mid-September into October 1918, during the height of the flu pandemic.

On board a ship with its confined space, the sick piled up in sick bays and appropriated other space, and still soldiers sickened and died. This nasty form of influenza produced a variety of symptoms, not all seen in any given patient: extreme pain; high fever; severe headache; delirium; bleeding from ears, eye sockets and noses; and, in many who died of associated pneumonia, a dark blue color that often meant death from lack of oxygen.

By late September and early October 1918, so many men were dying during transit to Europe that their bodies could not always be stored on board for land burials, sometimes due to lack of coffins. Instead, many required burial at sea. Some ships took extreme action to preserve the bodies—in one case emptying the refrigerator of food and placing about eighty bodies within it.

Into this mess in late September 1918 stepped Jennings and the men of the 319th Engineers. Their travels can be tracked from Camp Fremont in the Palo Alto area by train across the country to Camp Upton on Long

Island, New York. Toward the end of September 1918, Camp Upton was falling victim to the flu epidemic. From here, the men moved to Hoboken, New Jersey, for embarkation on a British troop transport ship bound for Liverpool, England. A letter written by one man on that ship indicated that the voyage was stormy and uncomfortable. Apparently, this ship carried the flu, and Jennings became one of its victims. A fellow soldier from the Redlands area, Corporal John Nicks of the 319th Engineers, wrote home to his mother, including a very brief message about Jennings, the first word his family got about his death: "Stanley Jennings, from Bryn Mawr, died on the boat coming over. He had pneumonia and had some kind of a hemorrhage."

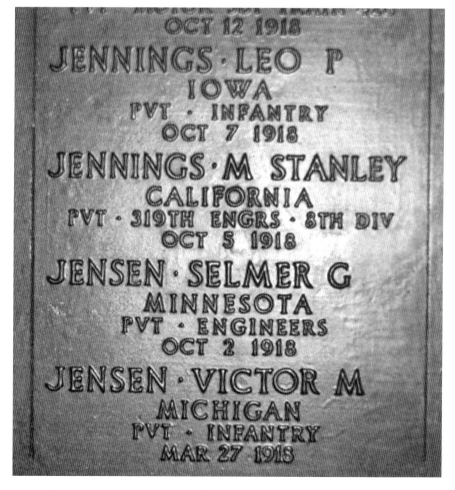

Michael Stanley Jennings's name on the Tablets of the Missing, Suresnes American Cemetery, France. *Courtesy of the American Battle Monuments Commission.*

This was the bleeding common to many victims of this flu. On November 11, 1918, shortly after the news of Jennings's death, the family received an official government telegram stating that their son had died on the ship on October 5. The family was anxious to retrieve Jennings's body for burial at home, but then the shocking news came that he had been buried at sea and his body would never be available for the family to bury. Jennings's name is cast in bronze with 973 others—some buried at sea, others missing in action—on a Tablet of the Missing at the Suresnes American Cemetery, Suresnes, France, just outside Paris.

Jennings's comrades in the 319th Engineers left Liverpool and eventually arrived in Brest, where they helped to construct barracks for arriving soldiers and then for those finally heading for home after the war's end. The 319th Engineers never saw combat.

Jennings death at sea from influenza presented a too-familiar scene in the transport of young men to Europe during the last months of World War I. No matter the cause of death, these men and women who died of influenza need to be respected for sacrificing their lives during war. It was war that sent them onto the transport ships and conditions of war that caused such massive spread of the flu on the ships.

U.S. MARINE CORPS

Many Redlands men enlisted in the army and were drafted into its ranks, but only seven Redlands men can be located in the records who enlisted in the Marine Corps. The marines did not draft men during World War I. All seven men traveled widely either within the United States or overseas. Two were with the very few marines at the Chinese and Nicaraguan American Legations serving as guards. Corporal Merlin Brown was in Managua, Nicaragua, from January 1917 to November 1919, and Captain Kenneth Schwinn was in Peking, China, from July 1917 to October 1919. Corporal Charles Truesdell served at Fort Crockett in Galveston, Texas, where the Eighth and Ninth Regiments of the U.S. Marine Corps stood ready to protect the Mexican oil fields important to the war efforts. He received over one month of training in a sniper school. Sergeant Earl Flory wound his way from Mare Island, California, to Quantico, Virginia, then to Rhode Island and, finally, to USMC Headquarters in Washington, D.C., where he served as a clerk, extending his tour to January 1921. Both he and Edward Hegewald, another marine, had worked for the E.M. Cope Commercial

Company before the war as bookkeepers, and in Flory's case, as a stenographer. Unfortunately, the three Redlands men who were sent overseas to fight perished in the war. Private William Carson was either killed in action or died of his wounds in the Soissons fighting in July 1918. Lieutenant Albert Simonds was killed in action during September 1918 in the St. Mihiel push. Sergeant Edward Hegewald died in November 1918 in the Meuse-Argonne Offensive.

U.S. NAVY

The navy did not take draftees during World War I, and its physical standards were tougher than those for the army. Despite that, at least one hundred Redlands-area men enlisted in the navy during the war. Some were in aviation, a few on ships ranging from cargo to combat and others served in support positions.

One man, Warren James, ended up on land in France working with fourteen-inch guns during the last months of the war. Ralph Cowgill, Redlands High School class of 1913, attended the school for ensigns in San

Left: Ralph Cowgill, World War I; *right*: Gordon Weller, World War I.

Diego but had not finished by the time the war ended. Gordon Weller left Redlands High School in his senior year (class of 1918) before graduation to join the navy. He became a captain of a very successful gun crew as reported in the *Facts* of July 5, 1918:

> *Weller was recently appointed captain of a gun crew on one of Uncle Sam's ships, and the transfer came after target practice at sea, when the crew made 7 out of 8 hits at a moving target at a distance of 2,000 yards, the ship moving at a speed of seven knots an hour in a rough sea. There were twenty-five gun crews to fire and the best crews out of this number were to fire. His crew made three well-placed hits on the target in the day-time and at night made four beautiful shots close to the bull's eye. Each crew were to fire eight rounds of ammunition (three inch) apiece. He is the youngest armed guard captain in Uncle Sam's navy.*

Weller returned to Redlands High School in the fall of 1919 and graduated in 1920.

The death of Silas Ballard, a signalman on a U.S. Navy cargo ship, was one of the most poignant among the Redlanders who gave their lives during World War I. Although he did not serve on a combat vessel, his work and that of thousands of others to help move cargo to Europe kept the American troops fighting.

Silas Martin Ballard Jr. was born in Texas in 1899 and remained there until he was about fifteen. He and his family had moved to Redlands by 1914 and made their home at 130 The Terrace. Soon, Ballard was in Redlands High School, graduating in 1916 at the age of seventeen (see page 71). Next, he attended the University of Redlands and was a freshman in the spring of 1917 when the United States entered World War I.

Ballard was not eligible for the draft as he was under twenty-one years of age; however, he could enlist, and on January 3, 1918, he joined the navy as a seaman apprentice. He was sent to San Diego for at least three to four months' training and on to New York, where he joined the crew of the USS *Chatham*, a cargo ship making voyages from the East Coast to ports in France, with each crossing meaning exposure to German U-boats. This was one of the many ships needed to move materials for the rapidly increasing American forces sent overseas. He became a signalman third class. The *Chatham* made a run to France from the United States with Ballard aboard, arriving about August 1918. He wrote back to his family on September 9 that he would soon be returning to the United States as the ship completed its round trip.

USS *Chatham* about 1917 (called USS *Margaret* at that time). *Courtesy of the Naval History and Heritage Command, photo #NH 105272.*

The USS *Chatham* returned to France with cargo in October 1918 and sailed into the port area of Rochefort, located between St. Nazaire and Brest, two larger ports. On Sunday, October 27, 1918, Ballard and his friend Oliver Uliverie, another signalman, had shore liberty and went into the town of Rochefort. The next part of the story is best told by the captain of his ship, Thomas J. Sammon, in a letter sent to Ballard's mother dated November 12, 1918, the day after the war ended:

> *They were eating dinner in a small restaurant in the town* [Rochefort] *when a commotion was heard in the street, and both the boys went outside to see what was happening. Shortly after they reached the scene a Frenchman, who was armed with a knife, made a lunge with it to get away, and it regrettably found its mark below your son's heart before he realized what was occurring. He received medical attention almost immediately, but he was beyond help, and succumbed to the wound in a short time. His body was laid to rest at Rochefort, France, with simple but impressive military honors, and the grave was well marked and registered.*

Here was a young man, just nineteen years old, who lost his life in France, not fighting in the war but through murder. He was buried in a French cemetery and the grave marked. This was important to the family, as they wanted to know exactly where their son's body was and, perhaps, later, to disinter and bring it back to the United States.

Ballard's mother received the telegram announcing the death of her only son on October 30, just three days after his death. The telegram was short, implied that he had died on the USS *Chatham* and gave little detail about the circumstances of Ballard's death. The letter cited above, from his captain, was written on November 12, 1918, and arrived at the Ballard home in Redlands by November 19, a fairly fast turnaround time for information in 1918.

But the family wanted more information. They went to their pastor at the First Presbyterian Church in Redlands, Reverend Nathan D. Hynson. This man would certainly understand their anguish, as he had two sons serving overseas. Reverend Hynson sent a letter dated November 22, just a few days after receiving word from Ballard's captain. Based on the later answer, the family wanted to know at least the name of the young man with Ballard when he died and more about his death and grave marker. Now came a much longer wait, over two months. A response was received on February 3, 1919, from the supply officer of the USS *Chatham*, R.J. Graff. Graff placed flowers on Ballard's grave in Rochefort, made sure the grave was registered for later identification and was also now able to give them more details about what happened to the man who stabbed him. A naval court inquiry had occurred sometime between Ballard's October 27 death and the February 3 letter. Ballard was exonerated from any part in the event that resulted in his stabbing but was unfortunate enough to have been on the scene. The inquiry also revealed that "a Frenchman had confessed the crime and was being held for further trial." At present, no other data is available to know whether this Frenchman was convicted.

Although living only a short time, Ballard had impressed people with his future potential. He graduated from high school at seventeen, went on to University of Redlands that same year and had expressed a desire to go to the Naval Academy in Annapolis should he have stayed in the service. Both his captain and the supply officer spoke highly of him, giving us another view of his character. Graff stated to Reverend Hynson, "Again express to Mrs. Ballard our sympathy, because without a doubt her son was the best liked young man aboard this ship, and I often hear the boys speak of him even now and wonder if there is anything that they can do."

After World War I, families who had lost a son in France were given the choice of having the body buried in a large American cemetery in France, reburied in a national cemetery in the United States or returned for burial to a designated town in the United States. The Ballard family decided to have their son buried in Arlington National Cemetery. His re-interment to Arlington occurred on Veteran's Day—November 11, 1920—two years after his death. Neither the first to die from Redlands in World War I nor the last, Ballard's death was certainly one of the strangest.

AVIATION

The same war that contained horses and blacksmiths also introduced airplanes into combat. Many Redlands men took advantage of this new

field, with fifty-one entering army aviation and ten naval aviation. Most of these men enlisted; only a few were drafted into the army and ended up in aviation. Although some were pilots and flew in combat, more were in ground service, including numerous men working as mechanics. Six men joined the balloon companies, including mechanics and truck drivers. These men in aviation crisscrossed the country for training from university ground schools for pilots to mechanical instruction. March Field (now March Air Reserve Base), North Island and Rockwell Field, San Diego, were used by many of the Redlands men.

Two men from Redlands died in the aviation service. Alan Bedell did not

Perry Haddock, football fullback at the University of Redlands in 1916, from the 1917 *La Letra*.

die while flying, but Lieutenant James Perry Haddock died on May 6, 1919, in a plane wreck in Texas after the war, apparently while on military duty. He was a former University of Redlands student from San Diego, graduated from the University of California–Berkeley aviation ground school and went on to train and instruct in the aviation area during the war.

The story of Alan Bedell, a long-distance motorcycle champion before the war and aspiring pilot, was not unusual—except for his early death due to disease. Although a resident for only a short time, Bedell was claimed by Redlands and accomplished much in his short life.

Bedell grew up in Montclair, New Jersey, and had appeared in Redlands by at least April 1917. By age twenty, he owned Bedell's Cyclery, a motorcycle and bicycle store and repair shop at 21 East Citrus Avenue. His was the local dealership for Harley-Davidson motorcycles. Only one Redlands residence is recorded for him, that of the Alvarado Hotel in 1917, on West State Street. He hired Roy Owen to manage the store and James Backus as repairman (the same man who died of the flu at Camp Bowie, Texas). This allowed Bedell the freedom to participate in motorcycle races around the area.

It was an exciting time for motorcycle riding and racing in the United States. Roads were often unpaved, bridges were lacking over many rivers and equipment was not as comfortable as today, but it was an increasingly popular form of thrill seeking and transportation. By mid-1917, Bedell was in the midst of this sport, setting records for timed races on motorcycles. His biggest feat was a 3,300-mile cross-country solo race, leaving Los Angeles at 11:00 p.m. on June 5, 1917, on a 1917 Henderson motorcycle. He arrived in New York City on June 13 in seven days, sixteen hours and sixteen minutes, breaking the previous 1914 record by about three days and twenty hours.

Harley-Davidson
MOTORCYCLES AND BICYCLES
The Cleveland Light Weight
Alan T. Bedell   21 E. Citrus Ave.

Bedell store advertisement, 1917 *Makio*.

Alvarado Hotel, Redlands, 1912.

One of the main reasons for the ride, besides trying to break the time record, was to carry a message from General Hunter Liggett in Los Angeles to General Franklin J. Bell, Governor's Island, New York, to experiment with the feasibility of the military using motorcycles to carry papers, maps and photographs that could not be telegraphed. After this cross-country record, the *Facts* of July 7, 1917, noted that Bedell became known by the name "Boss of the Road from Broadway to Broadway."

On October 2, 1917, Alan Bedell was not yet eligible for the draft, as he would not be twenty-one until November 1917, so he enlisted as a flying cadet in the U.S. Army. He started in Ithaca, New York, attending ground school at Cornell University for eight weeks. He married Mildred Cutter of Boston on December 15 in Montclair, New Jersey.

By December 25, he was in southwestern Louisiana at Gerstner Field, an aviation school where he would learn to fly. Flying cadets first attended ground school and then received six to eight weeks of flying training followed by more training overseas if headed to the European theater. Once finished with flying school in the United States, the cadets had to pass an exam to become a commissioned officer. Bedell mentioned flying a half hour daily with an instructor. He described some of his feelings toward flying in letters that ended up in motorcycle magazines of the time such as this quote from the *Pacific Motorcyclist and Western Wheelman* of December 26, 1917, as published in the *Facts* of January 16, 1918: "However exciting driving an aeroplane may be, it hasn't got the thrill of the good old two-wheeler. You're just sitting there at the wheel and have lots of time to think things over. Of course, if you 'pile up,' it's worse than spilling off a Henderson, but there isn't much chance of that if you're careful."

Gerstner Field turned out to be a physically challenging place in which to live and work. One local historian described it as full of mosquitos and blowing sand that gummed up the plane engines (and probably men's lungs). It was also overcrowded, with chronic sanitation problems.

By mid-February 1918, Bedell had finished at least six weeks of pilot training, putting him toward the end of his flight work. A reporter for the *Oakland Tribune* on June 17, 1917, described Bedell as one of "the most remarkable motorcycle rider[s] of today and his stamina in races...is unequaled." When he finished his transcontinental ride in New York City on June 13, 1917, he was described as in excellent health despite the grueling run. But regardless of his earlier good health, about mid-February, his wife and mother were notified by telegram that he was very ill at Gerstner Field. From February 13, he was under medical care; pneumonia would kill him on February 24, 1918. Sadly, his family arrived after his death. He was just slightly over twenty-one years old when he died. The *Facts* noted that his "numerous friends in Redlands and Southern California in general will grieve at his passing." Alan Bedell was buried in Green-Wood Cemetery, Brooklyn, New York, on February 28, 1918, just four days after his death.

Meanwhile, what happened to Bedell's Cyclery in Redlands? Roy Owen, manager, found out the hard way that Bedell had died. Owen read of the death in a motorcycle magazine about ten days after it happened and promptly telegrammed Bedell's family to determine if this was correct. By June 1918, his family had decided to sell his shop in Redlands. Roy Owen purchased it from the estate by July 1918. It is hard to say what other exploits Bedell might have accomplished had he survived World War I, but he certainly lived life fully during his twenty-one years.

So many fascinating stories exist about the men of Redlands who enlisted in World War I that could not be told in this book. They range from experiences in the United States to those around the globe. Whether in supply, medical, aviation, infantry, shipboard or other military fields, they all served their country.

4

OVER THERE

Redlanders and the rest of their comrades in the U.S. Army were woefully unprepared for the horrors that would await them in France. After a brief mobile phase in 1914, the conflict had degenerated into stalemated bloody trench warfare. In the succeeding years, massive battles along the so-called western front at Ypres, Verdun and the Somme did little but add to the staggering casualty lists. Against the deadly combination of powerful artillery, rapid-firing machine guns and gas warfare, attacking infantrymen stood little chance. In the most sanguinary example, nineteen thousand British soldiers were killed on the first day of the Somme battle, which would drag on for five months with little territorial gain.

503 - Attaque aux gaz - Somme -

Allied gas attack against German positions on the Somme, 1916. *WW1 Signal Corps Collection United States Army Heritage and Education Center, Carlisle, PA.*

Unburied German soldier. Photographed by Dr. John L. Avey on a tour of the front lines after the armistice. *John L. Avey collection, Courtesy of the Avey family.*

FIRST TO FIGHT

Several Redlands men elected not to wait for America to get involved in the war, instead joining the Canadian army, which was fighting as part of the British Expeditionary Force in France. Frank and James Purvis graduated from Redlands High School in 1905 and 1911, respectively. Frank's subsequent 1911 engineering degree from Stanford University enabled him to be appointed an officer in Canada's Royal Engineers. He repaired roads, constructed tunnels at Vimy Ridge and was awarded the Military Cross in 1918 for repairing a bridge under heavy Bolshevik fire on the northern Russian front. James, one of the Citrus Belt League's best distance runners, emerged unscathed after three years of extensive combat as an infantryman with the Fourth Mounted Rifle Regiment. Walter S. Ford joined Canada's Royal Artillery in 1915 and after service at Ypres was commissioned as a lieutenant. In February 1918, he was in an observation post with two other soldiers when a shell exploded nearby, killing his companions and injuring him about the head, affecting his hearing. Former University of Redlands football player Arthur Cocking left school to join the Royal Canadian Air Force in 1916. By November 1917, he was serving in France with the Eighty-Second Squadron, flying a single-seat FE8 photo reconnaissance biplane he nicknamed *Pi Chi* in honor of his college fraternity. In a June 1918 letter to a fraternity brother, Lieutenant Cocking described what would turn out to be his final combat mission.

> *About six weeks ago there was a job of photography on the Huns rear defenses. I was to do it, but at the last minute the OC changed me and sent me to do a shoot. The chap that took my place was jumped on by five Huns and shot down in flames. To be shot down in flames is our worst fear, a death of torture, and you know you haven't a chance in the world. The daisies would've been growing beautifully but for my luck....All went well until the big push, when I was forced to land near the Boche. They had shot my machine to pieces and I burned it to keep the Huns from getting it. One of the shells clicked me in the knee, and I'm here in England for a short rest.*

His nonchalant tone notwithstanding, Cocking was prevented from flying for the remainder of the war, apparently because of "shell shock," the World War I–era phrase for posttraumatic stress disorder.

Walter M. Clark left his dentistry practice in downtown Redlands in the fall of 1917 to enlist in a Canadian artillery battery. His first major action in September 1918 was almost his last, as he relayed in a letter to a Redlands friend:

> *A bunch of us got too far ahead and the Heinie machine guns were making it pretty hot for us....I got a machine gun bullet in my ribs and drifted back to the rear. How it came to a stop I don't know. It had a soft nose and flattened out. I walked out after pulling the thing out and putting on a bandage. I'm in a hospital, but will no doubt go back up the line as soon as all danger of blood poisoning leaves. Walking through a German barrage is no joke. I came near getting all the war I wanted.*

Roy Whiteside is considered a Redlands World War I death by all three memorial sites (the memorial plaque at Hillside mausoleum, the Jennie Davis Park wall and the American Legion Post 106 veterans list), but they incorrectly honor another man with the same last name, E.E. Whiteside. Other than this August 8, 1918 *Facts* citation, there is tragically no information about the circumstances of Roy Whiteside's service or death: "Another former Redlands boy has been killed in France. He is Roy Whiteside, and he enlisted with the Canadian army some time ago. He was only 19 years of age when killed."

One Redlander fought with the French in the famous Lafayette Escadrille. Charles Nordhoff was the son of wealthy journalist and author Walter

Nordhoff, who had a home on Pacific Street. After graduating from Harvard, Charles spent time in Mexico and then worked as an executive in the family's brick and tile business in Redlands. In 1916, he quit to join the U.S. Ambulance Service, assisting the French army. His experiences apparently convinced him to become a combatant because in June 1917 he transferred into the famous squadron of American volunteers named after the French marquis who had assisted George Washington during the American Revolution. After completing fighter pilot training, he was assigned to the Ninety-Ninth Squadron, spent six months at the front flying a SPAD XIII and was awarded the Croix de Guerre (War Cross) with Star for downing one German aircraft. In July 1918, he was transferred into the U.S. Army Air Service as a staff officer where, he would later write, "he spent the balance of the war in removing split infinitives from military reports." Postwar, he and fellow pilot James Hall would write the official history of the Lafayette Escadrille and a slew of popular novels, including *Mutiny on the Bounty.*

Arrival of the American Army

Perhaps the first Redlander wearing Uncle Sam's uniform to arrive on the western front was twenty-one-year-old Thomas Hynson. The son of Presbyterian minister Nathan Hynson, Thomas was studying at the University of Pennsylvania in the spring of 1917. When America declared war, he joined the U.S. Army's Ambulance Corps. After a short period of training with their Ford ambulances, Hynson's unit was shipped to France in September 1917. On the journey over, his transport, the SS *Baltic*, was hit by a torpedo that miraculously failed to explode. With only a handful of American soldiers in France and none of them combat ready, Hynson's unit was attached to the French army to assist with evacuating their many wounded. In a series of letters to his father, Private Hynson shared some of his impressions:

> *On the front we live in dugouts 30 feet under the ground. Just now the guns are hammering away and nearly shake the pencil as I write....What would you think if I told you I had not had a bath for two months? They used to say that "cleanliness was next to godliness", but here it is next to impossible....The thing that gets me the worst is the character of the loads*

we carry. Some of the poor fellows are pretty far gone and every bump in the road is a cruel jolt which I feel myself.

In March 1918, Hynson was driving in a convoy of ambulances evacuating wounded when it was hit by a German artillery barrage. The official French report of the incident stated, "Although his ambulance was blown from the road by the explosion of a shell, yet he continued on the execution of his mission, rescuing artillerymen wounded by the same shell, although he himself was beginning to be overcome by gas."

In recognition of his bravery, he became the first Redlander to be decorated with the Croix de Guerre by the French. After recovering, he returned to the front only to be gassed a second time, this time requiring a four-month hospital stay.

What had been a trickle of arriving American soldiers in 1917 started to become a flood as the new year began. Among these early 1918 arrivals were Redlanders Allen Whitney and John Stocker. Born and raised in Redlands, Allen Whitney graduated from both Redlands High School and the University of Redlands. In August 1917, he left his job with the Santa Fe Railroad and enlisted as a lieutenant in the U.S. Army, eventually serving with the 102nd Field Artillery Regiment, 26th (Yankee) Infantry Division. Just after arriving in France in March, Private Whitney wrote a relative about his first impressions:

France is a wonderful place and I am enjoying every minute. I haven't had a drink of water since landing here. When we are thirsty we have wine and when we aren't thirsty we have wine.…I have made the acquaintance of a young lady and spend every Saturday evening with her. How I wish I'd kept up with my French in high school and college. But how was I to know that I was going across the big puddle so darned soon.

To gain experience, newly arrived American units were given quiet sectors in the frontline. Quiet did not mean danger-free, as John Stocker would discover. Thirty years old when he was drafted, Stocker would eventually be assigned to the Eighteenth Regiment of the First Infantry Division. On the night of March 1, Stocker was with a group of men bivouacked in a barn two kilometers behind the front line when a German shell struck the roof. Fourteen men were killed and twenty wounded, among them Stocker, who was bruised and deafened severely enough to require hospitalization.

Organizing ammunition, supplies and provisions for an army that would eventually comprise almost two million men was a monumental undertaking.

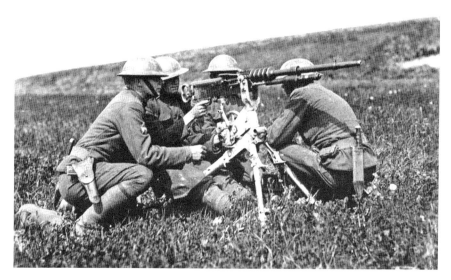

American soldiers of the First Infantry Division train with a French-made Hotchkiss machine gun.

Redlands truck driver Harry Beal behind the wheel of the "stage" he operated before the war. As a member of the 807th Pioneer Infantry Regiment, Beal drove supply trucks in France.

The men who drove the supply trucks that transported materiel from the railhcads to the front line played a vital role. Among these men were Redlanders Wilson Spoor and Harry Beal. The son of a prominent Redlands druggist, Wilson Spoor initially was designated as an engineer with the 42nd (Rainbow) Infantry Division when he enlisted in the summer of 1917 along with his friend Joseph Pray. In May, he was commissioned as a lieutenant and transferred into the division's heavy supply truck company. In a July letter to his father, Lieutenant Spoor described a drive to the front line during which he located Joe Pray and "had a most enjoyable time, interspersed with terrific Hun bombardments and a gas alarm." Despite being thirty-three years old, Harry Beal enlisted with the 807th Pioneer Infantry, an all-black unit in the segregated U.S. Army. One of the sons of Redlands pioneer Israel Beal, Harry had extensive experience driving trucks as the owner of a successful stage and car line catering to San Bernardino Mountains tourists. Initially designated to be a cook, Private Beal petitioned to take the trucker's exam, passed easily and was eventually promoted to sergeant.

Cantigny and Belleau Wood

In the spring of 1918, the war was entering its most crucial phase. Reinforced by dozens of divisions from the eastern front made available by the separate peace signed by Russia's new Bolshevik government and utilizing new infiltration tactics, the Germans had broken through the French and British lines and were threatening Paris. The most combat-ready American units, the First and Second Infantry Divisions, were rushed to the threatened sector. On May 27, the First Infantry Division, soon to be known as the "Big Red One," halted the German advance at the town of Cantigny, the first major American battle of the war. Among the participants was Private John Stocker, just recovered from his March wounds, who was in charge of two machine guns ranged on Dead Man's Valley in front of the town. An April 1919 *Facts* article vividly describes how he would receive his second wound during a German artillery barrage:

> *When a shell hit the parapet, Stocker was blown out of the trench and buried until only a part of his face and an arm showed. Soon the Germans sent over some gas shells and Stocker got some of the gas before a sergeant found him, pulled him out and put a gas mask on him. He was sent to first*

American Expeditionary Force on Western Front
1918

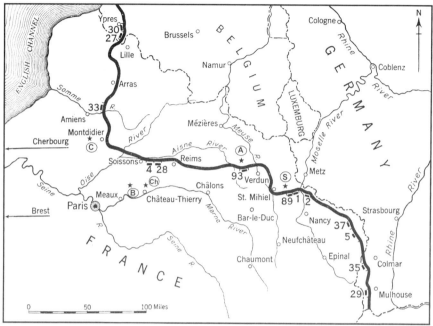

Map of battlefields in France, 1918. *Adapted from map* Location of American Division on Western Front August 10, 1918 *ABMC American Armies and Battlefields in Europe 1937.*

aid and there a German spy ran in and called to the doctors to retreat, that the Germans were coming. The head doctor organized his men into a line of defense when Stocker told him they had no retreat orders in the first line and later Stocker received the Croix de Guerre for going out of his line of duty.

At the same time, the Second Infantry Division—which included two regiments of U.S. Marines—was engaged in a costly battle with the Germans for possession of a small geographical feature known as Belleau Wood. Casualties on both sides were heavy. The Germans nicknamed the hard-fighting Americans *die Teufel Hunden*, the "Devil Dogs." Among the Marine participants in this battle were Lieutenant Albert Simonds and Private

Soldiers of the First Infantry Division advance at Cantigny, the first major American attack of the war. *WWI Signal Corps Collection United States Army Heritage and Education Center, Carlisle, PA.*

William Carson of Redlands. The son of the president of the Redlands-Highlands Fruit Exchange, Albert Simonds attended the Harvard Military School in Los Angeles and then enrolled at the University of California–Berkeley, graduating in 1917 with a bachelor's degree in arts and letters. That August, Albert joined the Marine Corps and was commissioned as a second lieutenant at Mare Island. Having arrived in France in April, Lieutenant Simonds joined the Eighty-Second Company, Sixth Marine Regiment of the Second Infantry Division as a replacement on June 14, thirteen days after the Belleau Wood battle had commenced.

Born on June 15, 1896, in Redlands, William Carson grew up with his brother George in a modest home at 952 East Central Avenue. Their parents, John and Mary Carson, operated the Lugonia Park citrus nursery at 21 East Citrus Avenue. When John died from asthmatic tuberculosis in 1902, Mary kept the family business going. As a boy, in addition to helping out at the nursery, William delivered newspapers for the *Redlands Daily Facts* and was manager of the Associated Student Body at Redlands High School. After graduating from RHS in 1915, he went to work in the oil fields of central California. When America entered World War I, both Carson boys enlisted in the military, with law student George becoming a truck driver with Company A of the Fourth Supply Train while Bill—as the family called him—waited until February 2, 1918, to join the Marine Corps. Private Carson arrived in Brest on June 8 and had a chance reunion with his brother George. On June 22, Carson was assigned as a replacement in the Seventy-Fifth company of the Sixth Marine Regiment. After twenty-seven days of harsh combat, the marines finally cleared Belleau Wood on June 26. Despite their relative inexperience, Carson and Simonds emerged unscathed. In honor of the marines' achievement, the name of the now devastated wood was officially changed by the French government to Bois de la Brigade de Marine.

Although the marine half of the Second Infantry Division garnered most of the credit for the victory, the U.S. Army half of the division more than pulled its weight. Private Alex Echevarria, who had fought hard just to get into the army, served with the Ninth Infantry Regiment during the battle while Captain Howard Clark and Captain Louis Palmtag both served with the division's engineers. A 1904 RHS graduate, Clark had earned engineering degrees at both Stanford University and MIT. Captain Clark would later write to his father, Lem, a former Redlands city clerk, that he was impressed with German military skill. "Without doubt the Huns know the game, there is no use denying that."

Nicked by a piece of shrapnel in the leg, Palmtag would become one of the 9,700 American casualties of the battle. Unfortunately, he developed blood poisoning, ending his front-line duty.

CHÂTEAU-THIERRY

Unwilling to admit that their 1918 offensive had failed, the Germans launched one last attack just east of Belleau Wood, at the town of Château-Thierry. In the way were the newly arrived Third and Fourth U.S. Infantry Divisions, including Redlanders Charles Rockwell and William Sanchez.

In 1917, Rockwell, the son of a Redlands telephone operator, joined the Fortieth Engineer Battalion, whose specialty was camouflage. In a letter from France, Rockwell shared his pride over a "first." "I was actually in the trenches on active work on Washington's Birthday [1918], and no other Redlands boy was there until a month or two later and maybe longer than that."

Attached to the Third Division, Rockwell's engineers were in the heaviest fighting at Château Thierry. In a July 22 letter to a relative, Rockwell relayed his experiences. "I have been in the thickest of the fight and thank God I'm still alive to tell the tale. But how we licked them and mowed them down and advanced over ground literally covered with their dead so thick that wheels of our wagons and guns ran over legs and arms of dead Huns."

Two days later, an exploding shell knocked over a tree, pinning Rockwell and a comrade to the ground. Wounded by shrapnel in the left thigh and

Shattered French town of Château Thierry. Third Infantry Division soldiers defending the buildings at right stopped the German advance. *WW1 Signal Corps Collection United States Army Heritage and Education Center, Carlisle, PA.*

suffering from mustard gas burns, Rockwell awaited rescue. According to a postwar *Facts* article, two men were killed and five wounded before Rockwell and his comrade could be safely extracted. Sanchez, a twenty-eight-year-old married farm laborer who served in the Fourth Division, was also wounded but nonetheless claimed in a letter to his brother-in-law to have thoroughly enjoyed the battle.

> *Well I met them face-to-face with my comrades and we captured three machine guns the first day. As we neared the Huns they threw up their hands and yelled "Kamerad!" I got their gun and played a tune on Heinie. I never saw one before but it worked fine, considering that a greenhorn was running it....I like the game fine, and I've got my share already. It is more fun than hunting bear in the far-off West, and more sport than taking care of the orchard in the east end of Smiley Heights.*

FIRST COMBAT DEATH

While the battle of Château-Thierry was raging, two hundred miles to the south in Alsace—at the very southern end of the Allied line—a so-called quiet sector would claim the life of the first Redlander to be killed in action. Twenty-one-year-old Arthur Douglas, the son of orange grower William Douglas and his wife, Lillian, was drafted in September 1917 and sent to France the following April as part of Company B, 128th Infantry Regiment, 32nd Infantry Division (Red Arrow). In keeping with American military practice, Douglas and his comrades were sent into the trenches in the Belfort gap on May 20 to gain experience. Technically, this area was part of Imperial Germany, as it had been annexed after the Franco-Prussian War. It had been the scene of heavy fighting in 1914, as France had unsuccessfully attempted to wrest the region back from Germany at the beginning of the war. In subsequent years, with more important battles taking place to the north, the entirety of the Alsace front had developed a reputation for being a quiet sector. The French had developed an almost live and let live policy with their German enemies across No Man's Land. That would change when the

Expended Allied artillery shell casings demonstrate the ferocity of artillery bombardments. Photographed by Dr. John L. Avey, a Redlands physician who served with the American Expeditionary Force as a surgeon. *John L. Avey collection, courtesy of the Avey family.*

Americans took over. According to the 32nd Division official history, "The 32nd Division found Alsace a super-quiet sector, and they left it anything but that. Soon shells were falling on both sides of the line, where no shells had fallen for months, and the front line trenches were no longer a place to spend a quiet evening."

On July 9, Private Douglas was hit in the chest by a piece of shrapnel from a bursting artillery shell and killed. In a division that comprised twenty-eight thousand men, he would be one of only fifty-six Red Arrow soldiers to be killed during their sixty-day stay in quiet Alsace.

SOISSONS

To take pressure off the defenders of Château-Thierry, Supreme Allied Commander Ferdinand Foch ordered a major Franco-American offensive designed to retake the important city of Soissons. Spearheading the attack would be the U.S. First and Second Infantry Divisions. After only a two-week

rest from their Belleau Wood ordeal, Private William Carson, Lieutenant Albert Simonds and the marines were put back into the front line. The first day of the attack on July 18 saw significant gains, but then—as often happened in World War I—the defending side was able to gather reinforcements faster than the attacker could exploit the initial success. Carson, Simonds and the Sixth Marine Regiment went into action on the nineteenth. According to a regimental history:

William Carson as he appeared in his 1915 high school yearbook, the *Makio*.

The 6th Marines advanced on about a 2,500-yard front. The ground was level, and contained no cover except for an occasional wheat field. This attack started in full view of the enemy and with insufficient artillery support. The accompanying tanks slowed the infantry. [World War I–era tanks had a top speed of four miles per hour.] *German artillery and machine gun fire decimated the 6th Marines. Within a half hour so many men of the 1st* [Carson's] *and 2nd* [Simond's] *Battalions had been cut down it was necessary to commit two companies from the 3rd Battalion to fill the ever-widening gap. The losses to the 1st and 2nd Battalions averaged more than 50 percent. It was almost impossible to evacuate the wounded. The regiment was relieved by a French unit that night and moved to the rear. The 5th Marines had enjoyed pursuing a demoralized enemy the first day. The 6th Marines had the bitter experience of trying to overcome the enemy with little more than their bare bodies.*

Among the casualties was Private William Carson, wounded in action. As described in the regimental history, there were great difficulties in evacuating the wounded. Ambulance services were supposed to be arranged by the

A French casualty is loaded into an ambulance in May 1918. The inefficient evacuation of wounded during the July 1918 Franco-American counteroffensive may have contributed to William Carson's death.

more battle-experienced French, but whatever measures they had taken were quickly overwhelmed. Although Marine Corps records would indicate that Carson had been evacuated to an SOS (Service of Supply) hospital, this would prove to be erroneous, as a subsequent investigation would reveal that Carson had been buried on July 19, apparently succumbing to the wounds he had received that day.

Tragically, none of this was known to Private Carson's mother, Mary Carson, back in Redlands. As the months went by, she became increasingly concerned as to why she had not received any letters from her son. In October, Mary elicited help from prominent Redlands citrus industry leader C.M. Brown, who wrote U.S. senator James Phelan and Congressman William Kettner, asking them to look into the matter. "His mother has not heard from William for nearly 7 months and they do not know whether he has been assigned or transferred to another division, nor whether he has been injured or taken prisoner."

Congressman Kettner's inquiry produced results in the form of a January 14, 1919 letter from the commandant of the Marine Corps, Major General George Barnett. Barnett informed Kettner:

> *The information that Pvt. Carson was wounded in action has recently been received at these headquarters in a delayed report on the muster roll of his company, but no cablegram information as to his injuries had ever been received at this office, which accounts for the fact that Mrs. Carson had not been given any information as to his having been wounded. The records of these Headquarters now show that Pvt. Carson is still in the 75th Company, Sixth Regiment U.S. Marines, and it is therefore considered probable that he is recovered from his injuries and is again on duty with his company.*

Congressman Kettner wrote Mrs. Carson a letter informing her of these developments. One can only imagine the emotions that Mary Carson must have been experiencing at this time. She now knew that her son had been wounded, but no less an authority than the commandant of the Marine Corps had stated that it was probable that he had recovered. A subsequent cablegram—which arrived only a little more than a week later—from Commandant Barnett must have been, therefore, doubly devastating.

> *Deeply regret to inform you message from abroad states Pvt. William Arthur Carson, Marine Corps, now reported buried, date and cause of death to be determined. No particulars are available, but see general information mailed*

Left: Joseph Pray as he appeared in his 1914 high school yearbook, the *Makio*.

Below: Private First Class Joseph Pray, 117th Engineer Regiment, 42nd Infantry Division in the trenches of France shortly before his death. The sign in the rear points to the "Boyau d'Uriage," a tunnel that provided complete concealment from German observation. *Courtesy of Win Lombard.*

you today. Accept my heartfelt sympathy in your loss of one who nobly gave his life in the service of his country.

Despite a thorough inquiry, the exact circumstances of Private Carson's wounding and death, and why one record indicated he had been transferred to a rear area hospital on July 27, 1918, eight days after his fatal wounding and burial, were never clarified.

Undaunted by the casualties, Supreme Commander Foch continued to feed newly arriving American divisions into the Soissons offensive, including the 42nd Rainbow Division, in which Redlands friends Wilson Spoor and Joseph Pray were serving. Born in Michigan in 1896, Joseph moved with his mother, Bertha, and his stepfather, Charles Lombard, to Redlands in 1897, eventually residing at 162 East Colton Avenue. A 1914 RHS graduate, Joseph joined the U.S. Army in July 1917 and after training was assigned to Company E, 117th Engineers Regiment, 42nd Infantry Division. (It was nicknamed the Rainbow Division because unlike the majority of American divisions, which were raised on a regional basis, its members came from all corners of the United States.) Arriving in France in February 1918, Private Pray sent several letters to his mother that would be published in the *Facts*. In one, he raved about the YMCA:

> *What makes us feel most as though we were still near home is the Y.M.C.A. There is something doing for us there every night. If there is no entertainment on for the evening, they have everything there for us to write letters, and a piano and a nice warm fire.... When we are over there again—"over there" means home now—we will not forget what the Y.M.C.A. did for us "over here." We all appreciate it and we hope that the people realize that we do.*

After a few days of fighting in the Soissons attack, on July 21 Pray wrote to his stepfather:

> *We have had another—and a real crack—at the Heinies, and if I'm not mistaken, those Heinies are feeling pretty sick about it.... They can't do a thing against us; our spirit is too high. Every time they turn around we just take another swing at them and knock them down. But their seconds shove them back into the ring. All we can do is keep knocking them down until they either refuse to be shoved back into the ring, or their seconds realize that it's foolishness.... What we want is to get those Heinies licked and get home—the sooner the quicker!*

Wilson Spoor wrote a letter to his father dated July 24 in which he expressed concern for his good friend: "All during the big push I was worried about Joe but I saw him today and he says he came through all Jake and that he got several good cracks at them."

Tragically, by the time these letters were received back in Redlands in early August, Private Pray had already been killed in action. On July 29, the Rainbow Division was struggling to cross the Ourcq River Valley against desperate German resistance. Although he didn't witness Pray's death personally, Wilson Spoor would later relate to the *Facts* that Pray had been "struck by a soft bullet, hitting him in the forehead." He would be one of 5,400 Rainbow Division casualties in just nine days of fighting.

Saint Mihiel

Concerned by the high casualty rates suffered by American divisions when they were under French or British control, American general in chief John "Black Jack" Pershing was determined to assemble all American divisions in one unified American Army under his personal command. With the Germans now on the defensive, Pershing removed most American units from the front line and planned a major offensive against the large salient of Saint Mihiel, which had protruded into the Allied line since 1914, resisting numerous French attacks. In the first major, primarily American large-scale attack of the war, 550,000 men of the American Expeditionary Force went over the top on September 12. With meticulous preparation and support, including 144 French-built, American-crewed tanks led by Colonel George Patton and 500 French-built, American-crewed aircraft, led by Lieutenant Colonel Billy Mitchell, the attack was an overwhelming success and the salient eliminated in only four days. It would be the first time in American military history that the terms H-hour and D-day would be utilized. The success of the offensive greatly enhanced the reputation of the American army to their somewhat skeptical French and British allies, who had been advocating that American units be broken up and fed in as replacements to their armies. At least two dozen Redlanders participated in the battle, including Edward Taylor, Clyde Cook and Albert Simonds.

Edward Taylor, a twenty-two-year-old former *Facts* linotype operator, arrived in France in July 1918 and was assigned to Company D, 103rd Infantry Regiment, 26th Division (Yankee). In an October letter to his mother, Ellen,

Taylor described experiences at Saint Mihiel: "I've been to the lines a couple of times and over the top....In one of our drives we captured a big bunch of Germans. Most of them were old men. They came out in bunches and held up their hands and gave up. Some who could speak English said they were glad they were captured."

Clyde Cook was one of five children raised by his single mother, Myrtle, at their home at 140 Calhoun Street. A member of Redlands Company G, Cook was sent to France in July as a lieutenant with Company B, Eighteenth Infantry Regiment, First Infantry Division (Big Red One). In a frank letter after the battle to his Redlands High School teacher Charles Latham, Lieutenant Cook delivered a sober appraisal:

> *You nor anyone in the states don't realize what the men are going through over here. War isn't like what it was in the old days; then they didn't have gas to fight against (and believe me, it is hell), T.I. cans (nickname for big shells loaded with either shrapnel or gas), treachery, etc. The Germans aren't very good sports either. Some of these square heads will yell "kamerad" and at the same time work a machine gun on us with his foot....Don't believe that the war will be over by Christmas; that is all paper talk. These square headed Dutchmen* [popular slang for Germans; the Dutch were neutral during the war] *are on the run, that's true, but they aren't licked yet. They know they are though, but their Hun stubbornness won't let them quit.*

In the killing fields of World War I, even a relative success such as Saint Mihiel was purchased with the cost of two thousand American lives. Among the fallen was Lieutenant Albert Simonds of the Sixth Marine Regiment, Second Infantry Division. Having survived Belleau Wood and Soissons, his luck ran out at Saint Mihiel. On September 15, while endeavoring to locate a position between the villages of Thiaucourt and Xammes to deliver rations to his men, he was killed by machine gun fire. He was twenty-six years old. The War Department telegram reporting his death would reach the Simonds family in California on October 2. The *Facts* reported, in the patriotic parlance of the time:

> *Albert Simonds Killed in France—Former Redlands Boy Has Given His All in the European War*

> *The Simonds family is well-known in Redlands, having been identified with the orange industry here for many years. A large circle of friends will give their sympathy in this great bereavement—a bereavement which has mingled with it a spirit of gladness that the beloved one gave his life in the service of his country, a service with which there is no comparison.*

The Simonds family elected not to have Albert's body repatriated, and he rests in the St. Mihiel American Cemetery. Albert's brother James also fought in France during the war, serving as an artilleryman in the U.S. Army. Upon his discharge in 1919, James moved back to Redlands and lived at 431 Walnut Avenue with his wife, Priscilla. In 1923, their first son was born. They named him Albert Carnahan Simonds II.

Under British Command

Although General Pershing largely resisted French and British requests to place American divisions under their command, there were a couple of exceptions. The Twenty-Seventh (New York) Division was loaned to the British, fighting at Ypres in July and helping break the vaunted German Hindenburg Line on the Somme in September. Serving in the Twenty-Seventh (New York) Division was Redlander Rolando Rivera, who went by the nickname Babe. The son of famous Redlands constable José Rivera, Ronaldo left his art studies in New York City to volunteer with the New York Division. Soon after arriving on the western front, Corporal Rivera was wounded in the left arm by a piece of shrapnel at Ypres. He recovered in time to participate in the massive British and Australian effort to crack the Hindenburg Line on September 27. Nine days later, he would write his parents a vividly descriptive letter about his experiences.

> *It was a drizzly dawn, very foggy about 5:30 A.M. when three blasts from some unknown whistle gave the final signal for "our over-the-top." At the second our artillery opened up I wish you could've heard it. Wow! I'll never forget it—I thought hell had broken loose. Well it was up and at it men, so on, on we went with howls and yells just like so many wild Indians.*
>
> *Of course about this time with Fritzies looming up in all sides with machine guns, to say nothing about many of my comrades falling on all sides of me, you can imagine I was pretty excited and mad. So I stopped*

a second, lighted a cigarette which gave me 100% more "pep" and nerve to carry on. I was leading a combat group of about 10 men. The corporal senior who was leading about 2 feet ahead of me was shot through the head, so I was ordered to carry on in his place. Twice before we came to Jerry's trench we were held up by machine gun nests and fights. Soon we arrived at his trench, puffing like stabbed pigs, jumped in, bayonets fixed, and routed it—ordered the dugout cleared. You ought to have seen the way the devils poured out, about 25 of them, that many about in each. Well they were sent back; we didn't kill any. We hadn't much time to linger as we had to follow our barrage. The way the Devils get down on their knees and beg and say Kamerad!

Well, I only got a quarter of a mile farther, as we engaged in a terrific encounter with the Jerries in a fight to the death. The trouble with the advance was that the Americans advanced too fast; some of them were killed and wounded by their own barrage. I thought we were going too slow but found out to my chagrin that we were far too much in advance, so we soon found ourselves isolated.

I tried to continue the advance but was driven back each time. Myself and another chap made a forward move from shellhole to shellhole. Zing! Zing! machine gun bullets sang past our heads—one struck my helmet, making a deep dent in it. At this time things were growing more and more serious with each minute. We made a few brief observations to see if we were near any of our men, but we were not. We were cut off and soon to be outflanked, and as sure as the sun comes up we were, within a very few minutes later. I told the rest of the men that we were in for a h—— of a battle and that we must be game and all stick together. No sooner had I said that than I heard loud yelling, singing and threats, and looking up out of one of our shells holes, lo and behold I saw about 50 Fritzies closing in on us, camouflaged with bushes and sticks around their waists and nearly each and every one of them had a machine gun.

There were only ten of us. Imagine standing off a mob more fully equipped than we, at a number of 5 to 1. In another second one of the many bloodcurdling fights for life was at its best. We stood to and let them have it. We had only two machine guns, but we held our own until all our men but two were killed, myself and a bugler from K company, so realizing our plight we hastened to retreat. We did and as I was going from one shellhole to one farther in the rear, the devil of a Hun shot me with a machine gun bullet in the left leg about 3 inches above the ankle, fracturing the shinbone.

The bugler from K company was shot in the left hand, smashing it quite a bit. By some hook or crook, they must have thought there were more of us and didn't come to carry-on, so we beat it. We lay from eight A.M. to 9:30 P.M. in a shellhole right in the midst of the Huns machine gun nests. We were found by a band of Australians, whom we Americans think are the best ever; they are wonderful chaps. We were taken to their dugout, kept and fed until the day after, then removed by their stretcher bearers.

Don't worry because I am in England now, away from the terrible war and having the best of treatment.

In recognition of his bravery at the Hindenburg Line, Babe Rivera was awarded the Belgian Croix de Guerre, the French Croix de Guerre and the British Distinguished Service Medal, thereby becoming the most decorated Redlander to serve in World War I. For some reason, Rivera did not receive an equivalent heroism medal from his own government. The shattered leg never fully healed, and he was awarded a 25 percent disability pension.

ITALY AND RUSSIA

Although the overwhelming majority of Redlanders who fought in what would become known as the Great War served on the western front, there were a handful of men that served the Allied cause in Italy or Russia. Induced by Franco-British promises of territorial gain, Italy declared war on Germany and Austria-Hungary in May 1915. Three years of stalemated trench warfare and harsh mountain conditions produced little more than one and a half million Italian casualties. Recognizing Italy's shortage of motor ambulances, an American Army Ambulance Corps unit composed of reliable Ford trucks and eager university students was shipped to Italy in June 1918. Included in this unit was 1916 Redlands High School graduate and Stanford University sophomore Edward Harper, who went over as a driver but was quickly promoted to second lieutenant in charge of twenty ambulances. Harper described some of his experiences in a letter to a San Bernardino friend that was published in the *Facts* in September 1918.

I am now at our front post, about two and a half kilometers from the front lines. The wounded are brought in on stretchers, carried by two men, and if the cases are severe the dressings which have been put on in the trenches

Lieutenant Edward Harper behind the wheel of his ambulance on the Italian front.
Edgar Hale Musser papers, Cecil H. Green Library, Stanford University, Palo Alto California.

are changed, then we rush them back to the dressing stations, about ten kilometers away. The road has been shelled, and the holes have been filled up with young boulders so the feriti (wounded) have a rough ride. When we are going fast from necessity in order to get the wounded to the dressing station quickly, and hit a large bump, they will start shouting "plano and retardo." After dark, we must go a bit slower, for no lights can be used, and the road is narrow.…We go back to the dressing station to eat. The food is very good. I am getting so fond of the famous native dish that I must have a big plate of macaroni to start each meal. We don't eat any breakfast, and it is so hot now that we don't eat much meat. As we are in the lowlands and the marshes we take quinine at every meal to ward off malaria.

Despite some close calls, Lieutenant Harper emerged unscathed and was decorated by both the Italians and the French.

Redlander Everett Dow joined the navy and served as a machinist mate on the armored cruiser USS *Brooklyn*, the flagship of the Asiatic Fleet. In 1918, the Bolshevik Revolution knocked Russia out of the war. The Allies attempted to give assistance to the so-called White Russian forces in hope that they would overthrow the Bolsheviks and rejoin the war effort against Germany. As part of that effort, troops and ships were sent to the Arctic ports of Murmansk and Archangel as well as the Far East Siberian port of Vladivostok. Dow and the *Brooklyn* were sent to Vladivostok to aid that effort, which continued even after Armistice Day rendered the original purpose moot. In December 1918, Dow was among thirty men injured when a coal dust explosion aboard the *Brooklyn* killed six men. After recovering from his wounds, he was discharged from the navy and stayed on in Russia, serving on the staff of the U.S. Consulate.

MEUSE-ARGONNE

The German armies on the western front had suffered major blows during August and September 1918, but they were far from defeated. With thousands of American soldiers arriving daily, General John "Black Jack" Pershing wanted to follow up the success at Saint Mihiel with a massive attack by two American armies, more than 1.2 million men, into the strongly fortified German lines in the Argonne Forest west of the Meuse River. A breakthrough would capture the important rail junction of Sedan, through which the majority of German troops on the western front were supplied. The attack began after a massive artillery barrage on September 26, including a battery of huge fourteen-inch U.S. Navy guns mounted on railroad cars. Among the sailors serving these powerful weapons was Warren James, son of Edward N. James of the Barton tract in Redlands. Despite the bombardment, progress was slow and casualties heavy. In the words of Pershing, "We were no longer engaged in a maneuver for the pinching out of a salient, but were necessarily committed, generally speaking, to a direct frontal attack against strong, hostile positions fully manned by a determined enemy." In forty-six days of continuous fighting, twenty-six thousand Americans would be killed, with an additional seventy-five thousand wounded. For comparison purposes, that is half the number killed in the sixteen-year Vietnam War in just forty-six days. Pershing ordered that the attacks be continued right up to the eleventh hour of the eleventh day of the eleventh month, when—per the terms of the armistice—the bloodletting finally stopped. Despite significant territorial gains by World War I standards, Sedan never fell.

Many American units were going into combat for the first time, and their inexperience contributed to the huge death toll. Among the units receiving their baptism of fire were the men of the 91st Infantry Division, known as

Ship Fitters Mate Warren James, USN. James was part of a small contingent of American sailors who serviced five massive fourteen-inch naval guns mounted on railroad cars that were deployed at the front in September 1918. With a range of more than twenty miles, the naval guns were very effective against German rear areas.

Soldiers of the Thirty-Fifth Infantry Division take shelter in a trench during the battle of Meuse-Argonne. *WWI Signal Corps Collection United States Army Heritage and Education Center, Carlisle, PA.*

the Wild West Division because most of its members were from California and the Pacific Northwest. William Bell, a former member of Redlands Company G, was sent to France as a lieutenant with the division's 362nd Regiment. Writing to his father on December 26, 1918, after censorship restrictions had been lifted, Lieutenant Bell gave a vivid description of the Meuse-Argonne fighting.

> *On 26 September we went over the top under a 4½ hour artillery preparation and barrage. The preparation is divided into two parts—the artillery preparation and the creeping barrage—the latter not commencing until the zero hour to go over. It was a magnificent preparation. It surely sounded as if hell had broken loose. At 530 we went over. I thought at the time that it was impossible for anything to live through the barrage, and I found out that it was about so. Everything was literally torn to pieces for 4 miles and we hardly saw a German, except dead ones, in that distance. In this we advanced our line 12½ km. From this on however, it*

was much slower because we were out of range of our own guns, and the Germans were opposing us with beaucoup machine guns. On the 27th we only advanced two kilometers and had our first taste of seeing our comrades fall beside us. We were capturing quite a few prisoners by now, and it was a common sight to see them running towards us with their hands over their heads yelling, Kamerad. On this day two of them stopped and put up their hands for me after I'd emptied four shots of my automatic at them….On the 28th we advanced 3 km, taking the town of Epinonville, and on the 29th had the greatest battle of all when we captured the town of Gesnes. Here our losses were very heavy.

He went on to describe an incident on the night of the twenty-ninth:

I wandered about no man's land for about two hours with Lieut. Lyons; by this time it was raining pitchforks so we decided to find shelter. I was about to open the door (of a house in Gesnes) and enter when to my surprise I stepped squarely on the stomach of a dead German. When I stepped on him it squeezed the air out of his lungs with a sort of wheezy sound which startled both of us very much. Needless to say we did not remain there long after that experience….It was during this time that a gas shell burst under my nose and after we were relieved I went to the hospital, where I remained for two weeks.

Lieutenant Bell was not exaggerating about his unit's losses, as he was but one of the 5,800 casualties suffered by the Wild West Division in less than a week's fighting around Gesnes. Included in the death toll were eight Redlanders.

Twenty-four-year-old Albert Edward Forker was one of two sons and five daughters of general carpenter John Forker and his wife, Josephine. Living at 114 San Mateo Street, Albert attended Redlands High School from 1911 to 1913 but is not listed as having graduated. After leaving school, Albert went to work as a truck driver with the Arrowhead Reservoir and Power Company in Little Bear Lake. After joining the U.S. Army, he was eventually sent to France in July 1918 as an infantryman and assigned to Company M, 364th Infantry Regiment, 91st Division. In the first days of the attack, Private Forker was wounded by artillery shrapnel. Red Cross representative Colin Dymen would later share with the Forker family an eyewitness account of Albert's wounding from a comrade in Company M, Private Arthur Vincent:

Albert Forker was wounded about 4 o'clock on the afternoon of September 28. I was thirty or forty feet away, but was among some brush and so did not see him injured. A lieutenant called to me to help carry him, however, and I got to him perhaps five minutes after he was struck. He had been hit in the head by shrapnel and was unconscious. We put him on a slicker and started with him to a first aid station, a mile distant. Half way there we ran onto a stretcher and carried him the rest of the distance on that. Upon arrival doctors said he would not live.

The Buehler family, who had a ranch in the Barton tract, suffered a double loss, as their son Omer, Machine Gun Company, 364th Regiment, 91st Infantry Division, died of wounds inflicted by a machine gun bullet on September 28, while their daughter Icle's husband, Caleb Pearson, 58th Infantry Regiment, 4th Infantry Division was hit in the side by shrapnel on October 1 and died four days later. As reported in the *Facts*, confirmation of Pearson's death came in April 1919 through the Red Cross, "the government having given the family no notification."

The other six Redlanders killed while fighting with the Wild West Division around Gesnes were Privates Harry Lefler, Leonard Haws and Howard Thornton (all Machine Gun Company, 364th Regiment, September 28, 29 and October 2, respectively), Corporal Amzi Jeffers (Company G, 364th Regiment, September 26), Private First Class Clement Raisner (Headquarters Company, 364th Regiment, September 30) and Lieutenant Paul Smith (Company M, 361st Regiment, September 26).

As related earlier, several other Redlanders had ended up in the 26th (Yankee) Division. Two from the division's 104th Regiment would lose their lives in the Meuse-Argonne. Twenty-four-year-old Manuel Marquez had been raised by his uncle and aunt Gerado and Miravel Bonillas after the death of his parents. A member of Company G in Redlands, he had accompanied his unit to the Mexican border in 1916 when Pancho Villa was attacking border towns. Sent to France in July 1918, on October 17, Private Marquez was hit by a high explosive shell and killed instantly. Ernest Richardson, a twenty-seven-year-old farm laborer who lived at 805 High Street, was also sent to France in July 1918. On October 29, Richardson was carrying rations up to the front line when shrapnel exploded just above his head, killing him. Lieutenant Eric Leroy Danielson of the division's 103rd Infantry Regiment, who had played "Taps" at Edgar Putnam's funeral back in Redlands in 1917, survived the Meuse-Argonne unscathed, yet somehow a misinformed friend from the University of Redlands, Private Herbert Chic

During the Meuse-Argonne battle, two soldiers from the First Infantry Division seek shelter during an artillery bombardment. Note the dead German soldier and disabled French tank in the street. *WW1 Signal Corps Collection United States Army Heritage and Education Center, Carlisle, PA.*

Hill (Company C, 116th Infantry Regiment, 29th Division), wrote to U of R student Alma Phillips from France that Danielson "had been shot through the lungs." As reported in the *Facts* in early November: "The young officer's parents, Mr. and Mrs. E.E. Danielson, 103 Stillman Avenue, have received no word of the wounding of their son, and were shocked when informed of his injury by the *Facts* this afternoon. The last letter they received from him was dated October 24 and stated that he was well at that time."

There were no subsequent stories in the newspapers about when and how the Danielsons were informed that Private Hill was mistaken and their son was uninjured.

Among the most celebrated incidents of a war conspicuously lacking in glory was an episode during the Meuse-Argonne campaign that would become known as the Lost Battalion. On October 1, 1918, approximately six hundred men from the Seventy-Seventh Infantry Division had momentarily broken through the German line and secured their objective at the base of a steep ravine in the middle of the Argonne Forest. Unfortunately, their adjoining units had not kept pace, and as a result, the unit was surrounded and cut off from supplies and reinforcements. For the next six days, the isolated men of the so-called Lost Battalion fought off numerous German attacks, including one featuring flamethrowers. Attempts by their comrades in the Seventy-Seventh Division to break the encirclement and come to their rescue were unsuccessful. Making matters worse, American artillery fell on their position until a Lost Battalion carrier pigeon named Cher Ami successfully delivered a message to division headquarters reporting the friendly fire. A written German demand for surrender was rejected. Finally, on the morning of October 8, the siege was broken. The Lost Battalion was down to five boxes of machine gun ammunition and had not eaten in six days. Over four hundred of the six hundred men were killed or wounded. Five Medals of Honor were awarded. The men's sacrifice was given great publicity and was the subject of a 2001 movie starring Rick Schroder.

Included among the units in the Lost Battalion was Company K of the 307th Infantry Regiment. This unit had originally been organized as Company L of the 7th California Infantry Regiment, which then became Company L of the 160th Infantry Regiment, U.S. Army, when the California militiamen were mustered into federal service. After being sent to France, the 160th Regiment was used as a replacement pool. The entirety of Company L was assigned as replacements to Company K, 307th Infantry Regiment, 77th Division. Among the members of Company L, 160th Regiment, was Private Francisco "Frank" Martinez, one of five children of laborer Alejo Martinez and his wife, Margarita, who resided at 204 Stuart Avenue. Although Private Martinez's military records were destroyed in the infamous 1973 arson fire at the National Personnel Records Center in St. Louis, it is probable that he was transferred into Company K, 307th Regiment, along with the rest of his comrades in Company L, 160th Regiment, and was therefore a survivor of this famous episode.

Regardless, Martinez's luck would run out only two weeks later, on October 23, 1918. The meat grinder that was the Meuse-Argonne campaign continued without relent. The Seventy-Seventh Division's repeated attempts to cross the Aire River were all repulsed. On October 23, Frank Martinez was killed in action, presumably during one of these failed efforts. The *Facts* reported that "no details were contained in the telegram, but as his letters home told of his being at the front, it is assumed he met his death in the trenches."

Soldiers of the Second Infantry Division operate a 37-millimeter gun in a blasted section of the Argonne Forest. *National Archives NARA 531005.*

The Martinez family opted to have Frank repatriated to Hillside Cemetery. For decades, Private Martinez did not even have a grave marker, until Ann Deegan brought this injustice to the attention of city clerk Sam Irwin and the American Legion. Thanks to her efforts, the grave of this Redlands hero is now appropriately marked.

The last of the thirteen Redlanders to be killed in the Meuse-Argonne was Sergeant Edward Hegewald of the Eighty-Second Company, Sixth Marine Regiment, Second Infantry Division. Only three Redlanders would fight overseas with the marines during World War I. All three would be killed in action. The son of a German immigrant, Edward left the accounting department at the Cope Commercial Company in Redlands to join the Marine Corps in August 1917. Finally sent to France a year later, Sergeant Hegewald survived the battle of Saint Mihiel only to be killed by shell fire on November 2, 1918, just nine days before the end of the war.

Peace

Their desperate 1918 offensives having failed, and having been hammered by an unending succession of attritional British, French and American attacks throughout August, September and October, the Germans had no choice but to seek an end to the war through an armistice. At eleven o'clock on the morning of November 11, the guns finally fell silent. Lieutenant William Bell of the Wild West Division, recovered from his Meuse-Argonne gassing, would later describe the reaction along his sector of the front line:

> *For two days before the armistice was signed there was not much fighting, as each side seem to realize that it would soon be over and to cause as little useless loss of life as possible. As the hour drew near we all got our watches and as the hand came to 11 we said: La Guerre finis. The French sure did celebrate that afternoon and night. All the cannons were decorated with flowers and that night they shot up their flares and rockets, which the night before we used for quite a different purpose. A great number of them consumed an entirely too large amount of vin rouge wine, and we could hear them singing all down the line "La Guerre finis."*

Sergeant Charles Rockwell (Fortieth Engineers, Third Infantry Division), having recuperated from his wounds at Cantigny, had the good fortune to be in Paris on leave on the eleventh and was thrilled to see the City of Lights once again resplendently illuminated after four years of blackout. Private Albert Williams (Battery A, Sixteenth Field Artillery Regiment, Fourth Infantry Division) expressed his joy in a letter to his parents on Clark Street:

> *I suppose you are all overjoyed with the news of victory—I know we were, although we did not go to Berlin to finish it. We were coming from the front after having been there for more than a month and a half, when we heard that Germany had signed the armistice that morning at 5 o'clock. When you're at the front in action you hear nothing from the outside world—people at home know more about the doings over here than we do.... Well, we are all wondering when we will see the Statue of Liberty with outstretched arms to welcome us home. I suppose it will be a few months before we are ready to go. Peace must be signed before they will send us back. It will be good to go back, away from the war ridden country filled with shell holes and dead Germans.*

Williams's analysis was accurate, as the first Redlanders who fought for Uncle Sam began returning from Europe in January 1919. Veterans Wilson Spoor, Harry Beal, George Carson and Leroy Danielson were among the Redlands men who accompanied the American Army of Occupation into the Rhineland to put pressure on Germany during the peace negotiations. Lieutenant Samuel Blake, a 1914 RHS graduate who saw plenty of action with the 368th Field Artillery Regiment, 91st (Wild West) Infantry Division, wrote to his mother, Ella, on January 11 about his experiences dealing with German civilians.

> *Tomorrow we are to try before court martial about fifteen persons for having government property in their possession. They have the habit here of taking blankets, clothing and the like, so we are putting a stop to it. There is to be no familiarity with them. It's hard to enforce that order though, for there are bound to be a few who fraternize with the soldiers. However, they treat us fine, and we treat them human, which is more than they deserve.*

After Germany signed the Treaty of Versailles on June 28, 1919, the final Redlanders who had fought, in President Woodrow Wilson's words, "to make the world safe for democracy" returned home. Captain Howard Clark (Eighty-Second Engineers, Second Infantry Division), who had been placed in charge of an engineering school in the interior of France after his combat experience at Belleau Wood and Soissons, wrote his father a "letter in rhyme" when asked to describe what the front was like.

"How to Know"

Where've I been and what've I seen?
Towns and such—that what you mean?
That sort of an answer's easy to give,
But to put it in words the lives we live,
The actual things we've all been through,
To picture—well, just gas, to you,
Is more than any one can do.

What is it like up on the line?
Have you got a couple of years of time?
To spend while I try to describe one fight,
And endeavor to word the matter right—

So you may know without being there
How the machine-gun lads and the doughboys fare,
Or the cooties go crawling everywhere?

How does it feel to go over the top?
I can shrug up my shoulders, but then I must stop.

Oh we know all right—as a mother knows
How it feels to her when the one boy goes
And doesn't return—as some of us do
And some of us don't—each time when it's through.
You'll have to wait till it happens to you.

5

WOMEN IN SERVICE

A t the outset of World War I in 1914, women in Europe and Russia responded with the same fervor and patriotism as their male counterparts. While unable to join the war effort on the battlefield, women across the social stratum mobilized. For many, this meant leaving the domestic sphere for the first time and entering the workforce. For those already employed, it opened new arenas vacated by men who joined the military. Women became rail car operators, police officers, bus drivers and many other occupations previously off-limits because of their gender. In addition to their new roles as laborers, hundreds of thousands of women also volunteered as munitions workers, prison guards, nurses and cooks for the military. In England, tens of thousands of women enlisted in Queen Mary's Women's Auxiliary Army Corps, the Women's Relief Defense Corps and the First Aid Nursing Yeomanry, serving as clerks, mechanics, nurses, farmers and receptionists. In Russia, many women were compelled to disguise themselves as men to join the military, while others enlisted openly after the formation of the Russian women's battalions in May 1917. In all, nearly six million Russian women of varied social and economic backgrounds joined the military during the war.

Such mobilization was not limited to women overseas. From the earliest days of the war, American women did their part to support the war effort, raising money, donating materials and traveling abroad to volunteer in hospitals, orphanages and shelters for displaced people. In many cases, these trips were undertaken at personal expense, without friends or prior experience to prepare them for the undertaking. With time, relief organizations, such

Portrait of brave war relief worker Florence Billings.

as the American Red Cross, Young Men's Christian Association, Young Women's Christian Association and Salvation Army, offered support systems for people who chose to serve in that way. These brave, self-reliant women left the familiarity of their home life to give aid during this global calamity. Among these pioneer war volunteers was Florence Billings.

A graduate of Redlands High School in 1897 and Stanford University in 1903, Billings was living in Germany as an English teacher as tensions mounted in Europe in the late spring of 1914. A chance trip to Brittany in the summer led to her being in France as the war began, and she immediately joined the American Hospital located in Paris. Founded by American expatriates in 1906, the hospital mobilized in 1914 and established an Ambulance Field Service to transport wounded from the battlefield. Billings described her experiences at the hospital in a letter written to her family in November 1915:

I've been regular as a clock there for a year—frankly speaking rather to my surprise. As I knew nothing about wounded I did no nursing, most of my work is in the department for making all kinds of surgical appliances and dressings.... [I]n our little hospital they had to use the same mattresses for a year—very badly infected men had lain on them, and you can imagine the smell....I saw a lot of wounded and it was interesting. As far as horrors in the way of wounds go I guess I've seen about the worst there is, short of those who die before they can be taken away from the front. I was awfully done up in the summer, not from the work, but from seeing and hearing it all. But I seem toughened now.

Billings remained with the American Hospital until late 1915, when she joined the American Fund for French Wounded, an organization focused on aiding smaller French hospitals and French and Belgian refugees in the provinces of Normandy and Brittany. Billings requested the publication of her letter in the *Redlands Daily Facts* newspaper and used it as a platform to request donations for the organization from the citizens of Redlands. She remained in France as a volunteer until December 1916, when she returned to the United States and toured various cities giving presentations about her wartime experiences. Speaking at a time prior to the United States' involvement in the war, Billings showed gas masks and other battlefield souvenirs and spoke of her time in French hospitals and touring battle sites.

Not long after Billings returned to the United States, the anticipated declaration of war came in April, compelling the country into action. People across the nation responded by offering their time and resources in any way possible. Women joined relief organizations, helped form war committees in the groups to which they already belonged, participated in fundraising and were conscientious about preserving resources needed for the war effort. Much like their counterparts across the Atlantic, many American women faced the possibility of gaining employment in male-dominated industries. With these new options available, hundreds of thousands of women applied for work to aid the war effort, only to find their lack of previous experience to be a barrier. Various industries established training schools for both new employees and managers who were unprepared to work with this new segment of the population. Colleges also began to develop courses aimed at preparing women for the workforce, bringing a more general awareness to the new roles that women would play in society.

Despite such social advances, there were trades that refused to include women. The Redlands office of the Atchison, Topeka and Santa Fe Railway, for example, openly eschewed hiring women, with an officer stating, "Girls are very useful on some kinds of work, but not for railroad work, where speed, accuracy and endurance are the sterling features" but conceded that "the more efficient girl, with plenty of training, would possibly be used here in railroad offices, if many more men are needed for war." This position by the local Santa Fe office is interesting given publicized decisions by the Baltimore & Ohio Railroad and Washington, D.C. street railway companies to hire women for positions vacated by men and pay them the same rate. In the first year of the United States' involvement in the war, over one million women gained employment in industries that were previously off-limits, easily disproving long-held arguments about women's abilities.

Women at work at Redlands Red Cross office during the war.

In addition to new wartime employment opportunities, many women in Redlands became active in the local chapters of the YMCA, YWCA and Salvation Army and were instrumental in the formation of a Red Cross chapter in Redlands in May 1917. These local relief groups were interconnected, sharing members and working toward the same cause. New and existing organizations formed war committees and began fundraising efforts with women in prominent positions. The Redlands Red Cross chapter, for example, selected women to fill twenty out of thirty-three positions as officers and committee members at its formation, including some of the city's most well-respected residents, and female "Precinct Collectors" were the majority in the initial fundraising and membership campaigns.

Besides the contributions that Redlands women made from home, at least two dozen local women served outside the city, becoming civil servants, munitions workers, nurses and relief aides. Most of these women were already employed at the start of the war, a statistic that was common at that time. Nearly one-third of them worked as trained nurses in the army, navy or Red Cross, as others joined relief organizations or gained employment with the government. The majority served domestically at training camps or hospitals, while at least eight are known to have served in France. Most of these women returned to Redlands after the war; one died while in service to the country.

In May 1917, President Woodrow Wilson placed war relief organizations under military control, charging them with specific tasks to approaching war relief. The YMCA was tasked with building up the morale of troops through "social, recreational and moral work." The group provided "educational opportunities, physical instruction and equipment" and organized musical and theatrical performances at their Y centers, both domestically and abroad. Y centers were established in military camps and served as recreation centers for men. These buildings were outfitted with rooms to socialize, play games and read and provided free stationery for soldiers to write home. As early as July 1917, the Y center in Camp Kearny, San Diego, had an average of one thousand letters mailed each day. The decision by the YMCA to allow women to join in July 1917 only expanded the services that could be provided.

Artena Chapin, head librarian at A.K. Smiley Public Library, aided the Y's efforts at Camp Kearny by helping to organize the camp's library in early 1918. Camp libraries were considered a vital source of recreation for troops at home and abroad. A founding member of the Redlands Red Cross chapter and a part of the group's organization committee, Chapin left the city in late March 1918 and spent seven weeks organizing the camp's library, which was one of the first of thirty-four camp libraries organized by the American Library Association's War Service Committee. The ALA played

Portrait of A.K. Smiley Public Library librarian Artena Chapin, circa 1918.

an important role in ensuring that American soldiers and sailors had books available to them. The War Service Committee received an authorization from General John J. Pershing, commander of the American Expeditionary Forces, to ship an average of fifty tons of cargo a month and was named as the central organization in charge of the distribution of books overseas. Interestingly, the committee was led by Librarian of Congress Dr. Herbert Putnam, who took a firm stance against allowing women to staff military libraries, arguing that the work was too physically demanding. The reality was that a majority of librarians in the United States at that time were women, and the Red Cross, YMCA and Salvation Army employed women in camp libraries throughout the war.

The Red Cross was made responsible for caring for the sick and wounded—a duty that the group was well prepared for since the establishment of the Red Cross Nursing Service in 1909 and the Hospital Service in 1916. The organization was also charged with service to American and Allied forces, prisoners of war and civilian victims of the war, particularly children, as well as with forming a committee to oversee the war effort. Established in 1917, the Red Cross War Council was headed by Henry P. Davison, a nationally renowned businessperson whose prominent position in the United States led to effective fundraising efforts and an increase in volunteers in the Red Cross. Estimates show that in 1917 and 1918, the group raised approximately $400 million and had the involvement of over 20 million people, nearly one-third of the population of the United States during the war, a staggering increase from 16,700 members in 1914. Redlands matched the national average, with over one-third of the city's residents joining the local Red Cross chapter. In January 1918, longtime Redlands resident Lena Dague was appointed as private secretary to Chairman Davison. Before the war, Dague was employed as a bookkeeper for Golden Banner Association. She answered the call of duty in 1917, joining the Redlands chapter of the Red Cross in July and working in Washington, D.C. as a civil servant in the months leading up to her appointment with the war council.

As part of its governmental mandate, the Red Cross was also tasked with establishing fifty-eight base hospitals in Europe: fifty for the army and eight for the navy. These hospitals were supplied with modern equipment and required a staff of fifty active and fifteen reserve nurses and twenty-five active and twenty-five reserve nurse's aides. With an early estimate that 5 percent of the army required medical care at any given time, the goal of the organization was to have one nurse for every two hundred soldiers. These nurses received a monthly salary of fifty dollars and were

Photograph of Lena Dague taken at Mutual Orange Distributors, Redlands, in 1908.

required to work long hours. The Red Cross Nursing Service recruited nearly twenty-four thousand nurses during the war, the majority of which were funneled to the military.

The U.S. government and relief organizations successfully utilized posters to inform and mobilize the public.

The city of Redlands had a relatively high number of trained nurses at the beginning of the conflict due to the Redlands Hospital Training School for Nurses, which was established shortly after the hospital opened in 1904 and continued until 1923. Located at 302 Nordina Street, the training school provided an opportunity for doctors to teach their nurses, ensuring that all patients were treated with the same standard of care established by the hospital. The program provided housing for student nurses while they studied and worked at the hospital. During the war, as the need for trained nurses increased, the hospital built additional nurse lodgings to accommodate their new pupils. Nurse training programs were commonplace in the United States in the years leading up to World War I, an outcome of the unprecedented loss of life during the American Civil War over fifty years earlier.

Among the earliest students of the nurse training school was Maybelle Wellman. A native of Pennsylvania, Wellman moved to Redlands with her mother, Louise, to attend the school about 1906 and graduated in 1911. After a decade at Redlands Hospital, Wellman left in July 1916 and leased Alhambra Hospital in Alhambra, California, where she remained for the next year. She joined the Red Cross as a nurse in 1917 and was assigned to the U.S. Army Nurse Corps, as were many highly skilled nurses at that time. Wellman received an assignment to an army hospital in New York, where she cared for wounded soldiers returning from the warfront. Established by the Army Reorganization Act of 1901, the army nurse corps had only 403 nurses on active duty and 170 on reserve in early 1917. The corps' enrollment swelled quickly thanks to the Red Cross Nursing Service, which added over 20,000 nurses to the ranks during the war.

As the war raged on, the demand for trained nurses increased dramatically, prompting Jane Delano, chair of the Red Cross National Committee on Nursing Service, to release a call to the nation's nurses to join the war effort in January 1918: "Nurses, and more nurses, if America is to win the war, is the cry of the nation to her women today.…Men are being called to the colors by the hundreds of thousands. Whether they will be protected and cared for when sick or wounded depends on whether American women are willing to make the same sacrifices their brothers are making." Those interested in serving were required to complete Red Cross classes in first aid, elementary hygiene and home care of the sick, as well as 240 hours training in an "accredited hospital." By May of that year, the nursing service had over eighteen thousand graduate nurses enrolled in the program.

While Wellman served domestically, Margaret Post went overseas. A graduate of Redlands High School in 1904 and Stanford University in 1908, Post was working as a nurse at Stanford University's Medical School when the nation entered the conflict. In December 1917, the Red Cross and

REDLANDS HOSPITAL

Redlands, California

MODERN HOSPITAL   **ALL CONVENIENCES**

RATES: Ward $15 per week

Rooms $20 to $30 per week

Maternity Ward $20 per week

Maternity Private Room $25 per week

.. Redlands Hospital Training School for Nurses ..

Information on application to Superintendent

The Redlands Hospital Nurse Training Program was advertised in newspapers throughout the state.

American Red Cross nurses at Naval Base Hospital No.1, Brest, France, December 22, 1918. *National Archives and Records Administration.*

Stanford Medical School mobilized Base Hospital No. 2, with the medical school's staff of seven doctors, forty nurses and hospital apprentices arriving in Strathpeffer, Scotland, in February 1918. Naval Base Hospital No. 2 in Strathpeffer was one of eight hospitals established for the navy by the Red Cross. Upon arrival, the navy appropriated four of the city's buildings, including hotels, to convert into hospital wings complete with surgical and medical quarters, a commissary and accommodations for the hospital's nurses. Post served in the U.S. Navy Nurse Corps until December 1918 and returned to Redlands following her detachment from the military to stay with relatives.

Another nurse who went overseas was Stella Harryman, who served with the army nurse corps in France. Like Maybelle Wellman, Harryman was a graduate of Redlands Hospital's Nurse Training School in June 1918 and worked as a nurse in town until being appointed to the nurse corps in August. Arriving in France in September 1918, Harryman was assigned to an army hospital in Brest, a city that served as the primary base for American military forces. It was at Brest that Harryman had the rare opportunity to interact with General Pershing. The meeting came about during a planned inspection of the port city by Pershing and his staff. The army medical corps organized a dance for the visiting officials and invited General Pershing's nephew, who accepted the invitation and unexpectedly brought his famous uncle with him. The general was known to drop in on his soldiers unannounced and take a keen interest in their activities. From among the nurses at the gathering, Harryman was selected to open the dance with the general and had an opportunity to converse with him after. Recreation for soldiers was an important consideration for military officials, and dances were a popular pastime. While nurses were allowed to attend officers' dances, they were forbidden from attending doughboy dances.

The efforts of nurses during the war were recognized and saluted by soldiers and civilians alike. In an issue of *Trench and Camp*, a YMCA periodical published at Camp Kearny, an article suggested that nurses be saluted for their efforts, stating:

> *There are thousands of men in this cantonment. Every one of them is dedicated to the task of upholding the national honor of the United States. There are also several hundred women here, and their tasks are just as arduous as those of any soldier who ever shouldered an Enfield rifle....Out on the base hospital these women are fighting just as valiant a battle and working just as hard as any enlisted man ever has or will. The Red Cross*

AN URGENT CALL FOR NURSE'S AIDS

ARE WANTED FOR SERVICE IN FRANCE—EXPENSES WILL BE PAID

As the war progressed, the need for nurses increased rapidly, prompting the Red Cross to advertise in the *Redlands Daily Facts* newspaper.

nurses are with us now, will be with us when we come back from the front line. When that time comes, and it is folly to believe that it will not come, the very life of any man in this division may depend on the services rendered him by the wearers of the badge of mercy.

The demands of the war impelled the Red Cross to provide other necessary services for the men in the field. In 1916, the organization created the Red Cross Hospital Service to focus on the rehabilitation of wounded soldiers. A canteen service was formed the following year to provide food, showers and laundry services to war-weary troops. It was in this arena that Florence Billings served. Billings, who spent more than two years as a relief worker in France early in the war, recommenced her efforts for war relief by joining the Redlands chapters of the YMCA and Red Cross. In November 1917, she returned to France, this time as a volunteer with the Red Cross Canteen Service. Canteens served over one million soldiers monthly in France alone.

Billings's time in the canteen service brought her closer to the front than she had experienced before. Writing from Chalons-sur-Marne, France, in March 1918, Billings stated:

> [A]*bout 11 p.m. I started for the canteen. The alarm sounded again when I was right in the middle of the bridge, and the guns began to go off.…[T]he bombs were falling around us. We stayed in the dugout about an hour and then went back and opened up the Canteen.…At 2:30 exactly, came the most awful noise I ever heard. It seemed right over our heads. The whole building shook, glass broke, etc. Right on top of it came a second and then a third explosion. I must say we behaved very well. One girl rushed to turn off the gas and electric lights and bank the fires, one seized the money, and I put for the hall to clear out the men, for you understand the Boche were undoubtedly trying to get the Canteen full of men, and if one bomb fell there in the crowd it meant a slaughter.*

In July, Billings wrote again describing the horrors of an attack on July 14, French Independence Day:

> [A]*t midnight the bombardment broke out, and you never saw or heard anything like it in your life. The front lines are only fifteen miles from us, and we were encircled by the very worst of the bombardment. We have often heard guns, but never anything like that. We were sleeping on our army cots and stretchers under the trees, and my cot shook with the roar and vibrations of the guns. We all woke up at once and rushed out into the open, and as far as we could see the horizon was ablaze with light—the flashes from the guns. It was like an enormous electric storm with red and green signal lights flashing along the forty-mile front. The French aeroplanes were passing over our heads all the time, very low, and we kept wondering if we didn't have German ones, too.*

She went on to describe the aftermath of that attack and the hundreds of wounded French and American troops arriving at evacuation hospitals nearby. That particular attack continued into the following day, and she visited a hospital to help the exhausted nurses tend to patients with injuries so severe that they could not be moved. The valor that Billings and other canteen workers exhibited was recognized, and Billings received the French

Croix de Guerre, a military decoration awarded for feats of bravery to any person, military or civilian, French or foreigner, whose name was mentioned in military dispatches.

While the army and navy had long established nurse corps, a variety of new positions opened to women within these branches of the military. For the first time, women were given the opportunity to enlist in the navy reserves in clerical positions, a change that had occurred just weeks prior to the war declaration. Citing the Naval Expansion Act of 1916, which allowed for the enrollment of "all persons who may be capable of performing special useful service for coastal defense," Secretary of the Navy Josephus Daniels formally announced the decision to enlist women as yeomen (F), on March 21, 1917. Daniels's decision was designed to free men occupying those positions for other areas of naval service, proclaiming that women would "provide the best clerical assistance the country can provide." The Naval Expansion Act was focused on building a strong naval infrastructure, including a large battle fleet. While the expectation was that this would only be open to men, the act's reference to "all persons" opened the door for the inclusion of women, an opportunity that allowed Secretary Daniels to advocate for the enlistment of women and ensure that they received the same pay as their male counterparts.

The navy reserves recruited 11,880 female yeomen, known as yeomanettes, in 1917 and 1918. Among those women were sisters Helen and Suzanne Graham, daughters of Edward Graham, founding chair of the Redlands Chapter of the American Red Cross. Helen and Suzanne both joined the Redlands Red Cross when it was founded and later joined the navy as yeomanettes. Yeomen (F) were expected to behave according to the same strict expectations as male yeomen and lived in barracks that were oftentimes sparse and overcrowded. Many of these women had no previous clerical experience and were compelled to enroll in night school to learn the trade as well as the naval terminology required to do their jobs. While a few female yeomen went overseas, most served within the United States, working as office clerks, commissary stewards, librarians, switchboard operators and a host of other jobs. Suzanne Graham served as secretary to the head physician at a naval hospital in the resort town of Cape May, New Jersey.

Positions also opened up to women in various sectors of the government, at times replacing men but occupying newly created jobs also. These positions offered equal pay to male and female applicants and required them to take civil service examinations, ensuring that candidates were hired based on their merits. Civil service exams were taken on the state level, with the results sent to the U.S. Civil Service Commission, which would then offer positions to qualified applicants. Many Redlands women took civil service examinations during the war, and several accepted positions outside of the city.

One governmental division that hired several women during the war was the U.S. Army Ordnance Corps. The ordnance corps was responsible for the distribution of weapons and ammunition to the army, a task that it was ill prepared for as the country went to war. In 1917, the corps began an effort to increase its production and improve its organizational structure. It was at that time that Janette Lever, reference librarian at A.K. Smiley Public Library, was offered a position as an index and catalogue clerk. Lever took a leave of absence from the library in July 1918 and departed for Washington, D.C., where she remained for the next several months. Over the course of the war, the corps went from handling six armories working on war production to nearly eight thousand plants across the country. Lever's term ended in February 1919, and she returned to Redlands for a short time before resigning from Smiley Library "to accept a more lucrative position in a bank in Los Angeles."

Lever's fellow Smiley Library employee Mildred Parsons also worked as a civil servant during the war. Parsons, who was first assistant at the library and a member of the Redlands Red Cross, was offered a position with the War Department in September 1918, prompting her to take a leave of absence from the library also. She departed for Tours, France, in the fall and was assigned to the records branch of the office of the chief quartermaster. The U.S. Quartermaster Corps (QMC)

High school graduation portrait of Janette Lever from the 1912 *Makio.*

was first organized in 1912, and it was responsible for supplying the army with food, clothing, equipment and transportation, as well as handling fiscal issues on the field, including compensating soldiers. The corps also oversaw national cemeteries and gained the responsibility during the war of managing cemetery records abroad. Parson's position within the corps was with services of supply, an administrative section charged with coordinating with other branches of the War Department and managing the duties of the QMC. Her specific responsibilities included cataloging and filing SOS records. She chose to remain with the War Department at the conclusion of her term and resigned her position at Smiley Library in 1919.

Just as men's war service created employment vacancies, so, too, did women's service. Emma Lederer, bookkeeper at the *Redlands Daily Facts* newspaper and former employee of Mutual Orange Distributors, left her position in April 1918 to work for the War Department in Washington, D.C. Lederer was chosen for the position because of the high scores she received on a civil service examination. A telegram offering her a job arrived at her parent's home in Crafton on April 11, 1918, proposing an annual salary of $1,100 and giving instructions on where she should report. The Lederer family's neighbors responded to their concerns about Emma leaving home for the first time by providing her with a letter introducing her to their niece Mary Swan, then a student at Washington College. Lederer was also fortunate that her friend and former co-worker at Mutual Orange Distributors Lena Dague had worked in the city since the previous year and had friends who could help her settle in.

Lederer was appointed to the office of chief of staff in the Military Intelligence Division (MID) on April 22, 1918, at a time when the MID was undergoing a period of transition. Military intelligence was an arena that had been neglected by the War Department in the time leading up to the war, and Lederer's appointment was part of a larger effort to reorganize the division. In all, the MID hired 173 officers, 23 noncommissioned officers and 589 clerks in Washington, D.C., alone. These staffing increases allowed the U.S. military to interact more easily with other governmental agencies and be on equal footing with other nations. Lederer's appointment ended on December 31, 1918, and she returned to Redlands the following spring.

Like Lederer, Freida Marti also served in Washington, D.C. A Redlands High School graduate and teacher by training, Marti took a civil service examination earlier in the war but declined a previous employment offer from the government. In August 1918, she accepted a position with the Department of Military Aeronautics (DMA), a predecessor to the U.S. Air

A snapshot of Emma Lederer taken in Washington, D.C., in 1918, while she worked for the Military Intelligence Division.

Force. Coming at a time when the field of aviation was still in its infancy, the DMA oversaw the operations and maintenance of military aircraft, including balloons and airplanes, and training aviation personnel. For Marti,

Lederer, Parsons and other war workers temporarily living in Washington, D.C., a bill was passed in December 1918 that would compensate those earning an annual wage of $1,400 or less for transportation back home until March 1, 1919.

Native Redlander Helen G. Fisk also did her part for the war effort. The daughter of Redlands's pioneer realtor John P. Fisk, she graduated from Redlands High School in 1913 and was completing her undergraduate work at Mount Holyoke College in Massachusetts when the United States entered the conflict. Fisk graduated from Mount Holyoke as class president in June 1917 and returned to Redlands, where she immediately became an active member of the community's war work, joining the YWCA and volunteering as a selective service registrar. Within a few months, in March 1918, she was offered a position as a "special investigator" for the women's branch of the industrial service section of the ordnance department in Chicago. The women's branch was formed in response to new considerations produced by the inclusion of women in the workplace. Fisk prepared for her role by learning the welding operation on manufacturing bombs before investigating the

working conditions for women in that industry. Her appointment required her to travel through Illinois, Indiana and Wisconsin, where she visited welding plants that developed materials for the military, including munitions, automotive parts and airplanes.

Fisk's report on the findings of her investigation discussed the importance of safety, sanitation, hours and wages for women in the welding industry. The report concluded with her determination that women were well suited for that work, even conceding that women were better suited than men

High school graduation portrait of Helen Fisk from the 1913 *Makio.*

were for certain types of welding jobs. She dispelled many concerns that were common about hiring women, determining that women would be a continued asset to the industry. In all, nearly nine hundred women were employed in military production in the welding industry during the war. Fisk held her position with the ordnance corps until December 1918, at which time she returned to Mount Holyoke for a brief period before arriving in Redlands. A few months after returning to her hometown, Fisk was the featured speaker at the May 1919 meeting of the Contemporary Club. In her talk, titled "War Time Changes in Women's Education," she discussed her experiences with the ordnance corps. The topic served as an indicator of her future in education as director of Western Personnel Institute, a cooperative of western colleges and universities, and as a member of the American Association of University Women and a trustee on the board of Mount Holyoke College.

The conditions that Helen Fisk investigated in the welding industry also existed for female munitions workers across the country. The demands of the war required the munitions industry to increase production, and the decreased availability of men led munitions producers to hire women at a high rate, a wartime necessity that already existed in Europe. In many cases, these women were exposed to poisonous chemicals, the results of which manifested themselves years later. Relief organizations collaborated with munitions producers to recruit a workforce for these jobs. The Redlands YWCA was a vocal proponent of war work, with the group's general secretary, Letitia Jones, taking up the call herself. Jones was a member of the Redlands Red Cross and a longtime member of the YWCA. From the earliest days of the war, Jones and her husband, University of Redlands professor S. Guy Jones, joined the war effort, raising money and recruiting people for local relief organizations. Jones was instrumental in lobbying her fellow YWCA secretaries to serve near the front lines in France, explaining that "their duty is to stand in the huts and pass out tea and cocoa to the men as they come worn and wearied from the trenches." While Jones did not go overseas herself, she did serve as a munitions worker in the United States, and her husband served in YMCA educational camps in Bordeaux, France.

Jones was employed at the Old Hickory Munitions Plant of the DuPont Powder Works in Jackson, Tennessee. DuPont increased its production of munitions during the war at the behest of the U.S. government, constructing five plants, the largest of which was Old Hickory. Jones arrived at the plant shortly after the first of its nine smokeless powder units went into operation in July 1918. At its height, Old Hickory had over thirty thousand employees and was producing 700,000 pounds of smokeless powder daily. The plant closed after the end of the war, and Jones was transferred to YWCA hostess houses in Camp Taylor near Louisville, Kentucky, and Camp Eustis in Virginia.

Hostess houses were built adjacent to military camps to provide a place for female war workers to live and for soldiers to meet with their loved ones while stationed at the camp. These buildings varied in size depending on their situation but generally consisted of a meeting hall, offices, a cafeteria, a kitchen and bedrooms. The establishment of hostess houses came in response to a perceived need to protect women who worked at or visited military camps, creating a "homelike place" for men and women to interact. They also came at a steep financial cost, which the YWCA and other organizations subsidized. In November 1917, the YWCA asked the residents of Redlands to help raise $90,000 to construct and maintain hostess houses across the country.

Hannah P. Hollabaugh, the wife of the Redlands YMCA general secretary, Milton A. Hollabaugh, also served at a hostess house during the war. The Hollabaughs left their Redlands home at the outset of the United States' involvement in the war when Mr. Hollabaugh received an appointment to oversee YMCA efforts at Camp Kearny in San Diego, where many local men received their training prior to deploying overseas. While her husband managed the Y base, Mrs. Hollabaugh's role was described as "mothering the hundreds of young chaps from all over the country who are being made into fighting men of the sea at the camp." She remained at the base through the influenza outbreak in the fall of 1918, which resulted in the death of twenty people at the camp and the establishment of a month-long quarantine. Cramped living conditions in military camps created an environment in which the outbreak could spread quickly.

As the turbulent influenza epidemic moved across the country, Emma Lederer felt its effects in Washington, D.C., where she and her fellow government employees were required to wear gauze masks and were banned from attending church services or public rallies. Lederer noted a decline in people riding streetcars during the month-long outbreak and quarantine. The epidemic severely affected the capitol, where nearly 30,000 war workers and military personnel lived temporarily. The sudden influx of new residents caused a terrible housing shortage in the city, with many people living in overcrowded apartments where the flu could easily spread. The outbreak took 2,300 lives in Washington, D.C., alone, a portion of the over half a million deaths in the United States. Hospitals were overwhelmed by the added demands of the flu, which took more soldiers' lives than were lost on

Europe's battlefields. Of the 236 army nurses who died during the war, most died during the flu epidemic, including nurse Maybelle Wellman.

Wellman was stationed at a U.S. Army hospital in New York in the fall of 1918 when the influenza pandemic hit the city. She contracted the virus and passed away on October 15, 1918, from influenza and bronchial pneumonia. Following her death, Wellman was honored in many ways. Her mother, Louise, received certificates honoring her daughter's contributions from the American and French governments, as well as the city of Pasadena, where Wellman worked before joining the war effort. The U.S. and French governments issued presidential certificates in 1919 to all who died or were wounded during the war. Perhaps the most lasting tributes to her legacy were the Maybelle Wellman Scholarship in Nursing awarded at Redlands High School into the 1970s and the Maybelle Wellman Women's Post, an auxiliary to Redlands' American Legion Post 106. Her remains were returned to Alhambra after her death, and when her mother passed away in 1936, Wellman was reinterred in Redlands' Hillside Memorial Park.

Sadly, Wellman's death came just weeks prior to the end of the war on November 11. Florence Billings, who spent all but one year of the war doing relief work in France, was still working with the Red Cross overseas when the armistice announcement reached her:

> *The men were quite happy. They all say the same thing, "nous sommes tres content." I should think they would be after four years of war, with so complete a victory....There are long trains of artillery coming back from the front—all with the guns covered and everyone at his ease. Each artillery man is singing his own happy little song and beams on you as he passes. Very different from three months ago when they were clanking up to the front, all ready to go into action. It is surprising how little enthusiasm or outburst there is among the men here.*

Despite the horrors that she encountered during the war, Billings was not ready to return to the United States. Remaining in France, Billings toured battlefields, including Verdun and the Argonne, which she described in graphic detail. Of Verdun, Billings recalled the road being lined in cemeteries and explained that the site went from having three graves to four thousand in the span of ten days. At Argonne, she saw a battlefield still littered with corpses and live mines. While living at the American Women's Club in Paris, Billings continued her relief work as a volunteer at a hospital for men with severe injuries, whom she said "smile all over when they see me."

—Buy Bonds—

LOCAL NURSE DIES IN EAST

Miss Maybelle Wellman, well known in this city, died this morning at the U. S. army hospital at New York. Until going into Red Cross work as a nurse the deceased lived at 40 Nordina street, this city. She was for several years a member of the Congregational church here and her name at the present time occupies a place on the honor roll of the church. She is a graduate nurse of the Redlands Hospital, class of 1911.

The remains will be shipped to Alhambra, former home of the deceased, where funeral services will be held and interment made.

Redlands Daily Facts headline from October 16, 1918, announcing the death of Maybelle Wellman.

This certificate honoring Maybelle Wellman was pre-printed using male pronouns, each of which was crossed out and changed to reflect her gender. *Courtesy of American Legion Post 106.*

As Billings's letters illustrate, the end of hostilities did not bring an end to the need for nurses and rehabilitation aides. In the days leading to the armistice, the Red Cross issued a call for 1,500 nurses' aides to be sent overseas, emphasizing that the need was present "whether actual battle is being waged or not." Care of war-battered veterans, many of whom had physical and psychological trauma, was a vital concern for the military in the postwar period. In response, the medical department of the army created the Division of Special Hospitals and Physical Reconstruction in August 1917 to provide physical and occupational therapy to soldiers, a task that President Wilson considered as deserving "more immediate consideration" than any other at that time. The division selected "reconstruction aides" to fulfill its mandate to utilize therapy as a means of rehabilitating soldiers and reintegrating them into society, a concept that was relatively new at the time.

Several Redlands women are known to have focused their efforts in this field. Army nurse Stella Harryman continued to work at a base hospital in Brest, France, until September 1919. Army nurse Marie Dufour served in Base Hospital Unit 35 in Mar-sur-Allier, France, throughout 1918 and took a position working with veterans in the U.S. Soldiers Hospital in Palo Alto in 1919. YMCA volunteer Hannah Hollabaugh continued to work with returning veterans at Camp Kearny until December 1919, when she and her husband returned to their home in Redlands. Red Cross nurse Ramona Jordan, a recent graduate of the Redlands Hospital Nurse Training School, arrived at Camp Kearny late in 1918 and remained in the convalescent hospital into the postwar period. Letitia Jones continued to serve as YWCA secretary at Camp Eustis in Virginia until her husband's return from France in August 1919. Another YWCA secretary, Ethel Amis, received her appointment to go overseas with the Red Cross after the war had ended, leaving for France in May 1919.

Margaret Sanborn, the daughter of one of Redlands's earliest physicians, Christopher A. Sanborn, was also a postwar reconstruction aide. After dedicating her time to the local Red Cross chapter in the early years of the war, with which she served as the secretary in charge of the Redlands headquarters, Sanborn departed for New York in the spring of 1918 to aid the war effort from there. In late October 1918, just prior to the armistice, Sanborn received an appointment with the medical department of the army to Orthopedic Base Hospital 157 in France to rehabilitate injured soldiers. Sanborn returned to Redlands when her appointment with the medical department came to a close and lived out her life as an active member of the community.

Florence Billings also served as an aide in postwar France, which she vividly described in a letter to her family:

> *It is a French hospital for one kind of case only, i.e., men wounded in the spinal column. It is in the Invalides (Napoleon's Tomb) and the men there will be looked after all their lives....One ward upstairs has all the absolutely hopeless cases. No one of them ever leaves his bed and they die four or five a week, but new ones come from all over France....That whole room is ghastly. I have pretty good nerves for such things but I declare I think of them the last thing at night and the first in the morning. It is worse than the war.*

Billings remained in France until November 1919, when she was offered a position with the American School for Girls located in Broussa, Turkey. It was in Turkey that she became involved with Near East Relief (NER), a humanitarian organization focused on providing aid following the devastation of the Armenian genocide, which had begun in 1915. Remaining in Turkey until 1923, Billings endured the effects of the Turkish War of Independence, which took place between 1919 and 1923, and became a friend and confidante to Turkish Nationalist leader Mustafa Kemal Atatürk and Turkish feminist, writer and political leader Halidé Edib Adivar.

MARGARET SANBORN

High school graduation portrait of reconstruction aide Margaret Sanborn from the 1909 *Makio*.

By the time she left NER in 1923, she was the principal female representative of the organization and, at times, the only American in the region. On her return to the United States, Billings continued to travel the world, oftentimes in the company of her sisters, Charlotte, Anna and Emily. She received a master of arts from Columbia in 1927 and lived the rest of her life in Redlands, residing at the Wissahickon Inn. She was an active member of the community, serving with the American Association of University Women and the Contemporary Club. She died in September 1959 and is buried in Hillside Memorial Park.

For many women, contributing to the war effort provided a sense of freedom and adventure that would have been unthinkable before the war. Ruth Durkee, editor of the University of Southern California's *Daily Trojan*, wrote of her visit to Camp Kearny during the war, "Here I was, just becoming reconciled to being a woman all my life, when along came the army and upset my equilibrium." Of course, Durkee's adventure did not take her to France, where Florence Billings faced the danger of daily bombardments or where Stella Harryman saw the horrors of wounded men arriving from the battlefield. She did not see the physiological aftermath of war as Margaret Sanborn and Marie Dufour did as reconstruction aides or the physical destruction of cities in France and Belgium that stood in the way of competing armies. For these women, the adventure and freedom came at an unexpected price.

While the war had a devastating effect on this generation of women, it also brought them closer to a future where their gender was less of a barrier. In fact, the sacrifices that women made during World War I were instrumental in the passage of the Nineteenth Amendment to the Constitution in 1920, which gave women nationwide the right to vote. President Wilson famously endorsed suffrage for women in a speech to Congress on September 30, 1918, stating, "We have made partners of the women in this war....Shall we admit them only to a partnership of suffering and sacrifice and toil and not to a partnership of privilege and right?...The women of America are too noble and too intelligent and too devoted to be slackers whether you give or withhold this thing that is mere justice....Many may deny its validity, if they choose, but no one can brush aside or answer the argument upon which it is based."

6

NOT FORGOTTEN

POSTWAR BURIALS AND MEMORIALS

World War I did not end for everyone on November 11, 1918. Some wounded men languished for decades, eventually dying from their injuries. Other families had to make decisions about where their sons or husbands would be buried if they had died overseas. Reburials back to the United States continued into the 1920s. Towns grappled with how best to memorialize those who lost their lives and thank their veterans. Finally, some of the mothers and widows who lost their loved ones and opted to leave them buried in an American cemetery overseas went on pilgrimages, at government expense, to the graves from 1930 to 1933.

After World War I, the U.S. government provided families three options for burial of their son or husband who died overseas. The body could be shipped back to the United States to the family's desired location, often their hometown cemetery, could be brought back to a national cemetery or could be buried in one of the American cemeteries developed in Europe after 1918.

REBURIALS

Delays in returning the bodies occurred due to the reluctance of the French government to release them, citing lack of transportation, health issues due to exhumations and fears that the French would object to American dead being relocated before their men were. An agreement was finally reached with the French government, and the first bodies were repatriated in late 1920. Over forty-five thousand were shipped back to the United States for burial.

The bodies of thirteen of the twenty-four Redlands area men who died in service overseas were brought back to the United States, seven to Redlands, two to Arlington National Cemetery and four to other cemeteries. Seven were buried in Redlands' Hillside Memorial Park, arriving from mid-September 1921 through late January 1922. Originally buried in France, they were disinterred and shipped to East Coast ports. The funerals must have been a sad time for the town, with conflicting emotions of exhaustion from the war effort, gratitude that the war had ended and sorrow over the loss of the local men. These funerals varied in size, with some drawing crowds of several thousand. Burials were scattered around Hillside Memorial Park, some in family plots and others in the new Veteran's Circle.

Albert Forker's body was the first returned to Redlands from France. His funeral took place on September 18, 1921, nearly three years after he died from his wounds on October 1, 1918. The newly formed Redlands American Legion Post 106 (created in 1919) took charge of his burial ceremony, as it did for many of the others. The body was escorted to the Redlands Amphitheater (now the Redlands Bowl) from the Dow and Fitzsimmons funeral chapel at 259 Cajon Avenue at 2:00 p.m. by American Legion men, a color guard, a firing squad, a Grand Army fife and drum corps and pallbearers from among his Redlands High School class. About two thousand people attended this first reburial ceremony. As the *Facts* reported on September 19, 1921, "[T]he military casket, of copper steel, was placed on a pedestal and the American flag draped over it. The flag was also placed upright beside the casket and flowers banked in front and on a table back of it." After a ceremony with speakers and music, the body was taken back to the funeral home and driven up to Hillside Memorial Park for a military burial.

The bodies of Omer Buehler (died of wounds received in action September 28, 1918, in the Argonne) and Ernest Richardson (killed in action October 29, 1918, in the Argonne) arrived from France at Hoboken, New Jersey, in mid-September 1921 and were then shipped to Redlands. Three years after their deaths, a joint funeral service was held in Redlands on October 2, 1921. Descriptions mentioned that the First Methodist Church was filled for the funeral service, with Buehler's father, brothers and sisters present along with a brother and sister of Richardson's. A procession of American Legion members, the Redlands High School band, a color guard and the firing squad moved with the two bodies from Cortner Bros.

Albert Forker's grave marker, Hillside Memorial Park, Redlands, California. *Courtesy of Ann Deegan.*

funeral home at Sixth Street and East Olive Avenue, Redlands, to the First Methodist Church at One East Olive Avenue. According to the *Facts*, within the church, "The caskets were placed below the pulpit, draped with the American flag and banked round with a wealth of beautiful flowers." The ceremony included a sermon and music and for Buehler, words from his machine gun company commander, Captain Brinkop, who "spoke feelingly of the bravery of the boy whose body was in the church. He said that Buehler was the highest type of American soldier, courageous but not foolhardy, that he was obedient and did his full duty and more too." Richardson was said by a *Facts* reporter to be "carrying food from the back areas to the men at the front…when shrapnel exploded just above his head and he was killed." The Redlands American Legion Post performed the ceremony at the cemetery and a firing squad honored the men.

Each ceremony for the returning men was different. The body of Frank Martinez (killed in action on October 23, 1918, in France) arrived in Redlands around October 26, 1921. According to the *San Bernardino County Sun*, "No previous announcement had been received of its coming

Interior of Redlands First Methodist Church, One East Olive Avenue, Redlands, California about 1905.

either by his family or the American Legion." However, the local Redlands American Legion immediately sprang into action and handled the funeral arrangements. Martinez's funeral was on October 28 at 3:00 p.m. at Sacred Heart Church at West Olive Avenue and Eureka Street in Redlands, with men from the local American Legion present. Martinez was the first man to be buried in the new Veteran's Circle in Hillside Memorial Park.

The fifth man to be reburied, Arthur Douglas, had been the first Redlands man to be killed in action in France (on July 9, 1918). His body was reburied on November 11, 1921, Armistice Day (now called Veteran's Day). This allowed the town to acknowledge both Douglas's sacrifice and the end of the war. At 10:30 a.m., his body was brought on a caisson and limber from Cortner Bros. funeral home to the Redlands Amphitheater by the local American Legion men. Although no photos have been found of the event, a *Facts* reporter's eyewitness description is vivid:

UNITED STATES GOVERNMENT
WAR DEPARTMENT
QUARTERMASTER CORPS
GRAVES REGISTRATION SERVICE
PIER 2 HOBOKEN N. J.

ecw   October 8th, 1921.

TRANSPORTATION OF CORPSE

PERMISSION IS HEREBY GRANTED TO CONVEY THE BODY OF THE FOLLOWING NAMED PERSON, WHO DIED OVERSEAS IN THE SERVICE OF THE UNITED STATES, FROM HOBOKEN, N. J. TO REDLANDS, CALIFORNIA.
AND SOLDIER ESCORT IS HEREBY AUTHORIZED TO ACCOMPANY SAID BODY IN TRANSIT.

FULL NAME OF DECEASED   MARTINEZ, Frank, Pvt., 3132510, Co.L, 160th Inf

CAUSE OF DEATH   K/A   DATE OF DEATH   10/23/18

DEATH OCCURRED ON DATE STATED ABOVE WHILE SERVING WITH THE UNITED STATES ARMY IN FRANCE.

BODY DISINTERRED BY THE UNITED STATES GOVERNMENT IN FRANCE.

THIS BODY HAS BEEN PREPARED IN ACCORDANCE WITH THE REGULATIONS OF THE DEPARTMENT OF HEALTH OF THE STATE OF NEW JERSEY, AND THE ISSUANCE OF THIS PERMIT HAS BEEN APPROVED BY THE SAID DEPARTMENT.

Interred - Hillside Cemetery Oct 28. 1921

R. E. SHANNON,
CAPTAIN, Q.M.C., U.S.A.,
OFFICER IN CHARGE.

Transportation of Corpse form for Frank Martinez.

First came the color squad with Capt. E.L. Danielson carrying the flag, being flanked by a marine and a soldier. Back of the color squad came the Redlands high school band, playing a funeral dirge. Next came the body with the guard of three soldiers and three navy men. Following this came members of the Legion and then the men who served in France with the various relief associations. At the amphitheater the body was placed on the rack in front of the band stand. Massed around it were the flowers which had been arranged by the members of the Women's Relief corps. The color squad placed the colors at the head of the casket.

Apparently an ecumenical service, Monsignor Thomas Fitzgerald of Sacred Heart Catholic Church gave the invocation while Reverend Nathan D. Hynson of the First Presbyterian Church, gave the sermon.

He [Reverend Hynson] *said that his hands rested on the casket containing the mortal remains of the first Redlands boy to make the supreme sacrifice, Arthur William Douglas. Mr. Douglas was 21 years old when he entered the service, leaving here* [Redlands] *on September 19, 1917, and going to Camp Lewis for training. On April 6, 1918 he sailed for France, after being at Camp Lewis about six months. He was killed in action on July 9* [1918], *being shot through the breast by a piece of shrapnel.*

The ceremony concluded at the Veteran's Circle in Hillside Memorial Park, where Douglas was laid to rest.

Caleb Pearson was the sixth man to be reburied. This was the man who married Icle Buehler, the same woman who also lost her brother Omer Buehler (whose reburial ceremony has already been described). The burial took place on January 8, 1922, about two months after the large Armistice Day funeral for Douglas. As stated by the *Facts*:

He was wounded in the arm in one of the earlier battles of the Argonne Forest, but stayed with his command, only to be more seriously wounded a little later, being struck in the side with a piece of shrapnel. Death followed soon. The remains were interred on the field of battle, temporarily, later to be removed to the national cemetery for American soldiers in France.

Pearson's service was at the Redlands First Baptist Church at Cajon Street and West Olive Avenue, officiated by Reverend S. Fraser Langford on January 8, 1922. The local American Legion men ran the funeral at the cemetery as described in the *Facts*. "Post Commander Raymond Hornby read the ritual at the grave, the choir of the Holiness church sang, and the firing squad fired three volleys over the casket while Frank Reinsch, bugler of the Legion, played 'Taps.'"

Whether the town was aware of it or not, the final reburial was for Joseph Pray, one of the first men to go overseas to fight and whose death on July 29, 1918, was also one of the first in battle. The funeral for Pray at Trinity Episcopal Church in Redlands at West Fern Avenue and Fourth Street included twenty men from the 117th Engineers who fought with him in France. These men came from Los Angeles to attend and brought with them the regimental colors that had flown in France. Several of Pray's military comrades still resided in Redlands, including Wilson Spoor, who had constantly tracked him down at the front lines in France to visit with him. Spoor wrote many letters back to his parents in Redlands that made their way into the *Facts*, keeping residents aware of both his and Pray's work. Spoor related to a friend in October 1918 that three months after Pray's death the hurt still lingered: "Since the death of Joe Pray, his companion, he [Wilson Spoor] says that he

is at times lonesome even amid so much activity." Spoor's duty at the funeral was as one of the pallbearers. The funeral service occurred at 2:30 p.m., after the body had been brought from Dow and Fitzsimmons funeral home by an impressive caisson and limber with four white horses. This was accompanied by the Redlands High School band. It was commented on in the *Facts* that the "music was especially good, being arranged by Harl McDonald in honor of the brave lad, who was once a member of the choir at Trinity church."

Joseph Pray, World War I.
Courtesy of Alison, Eric and Leighton Paul.

Edward Hegewald's grave marker, Arlington National Cemetery, Virginia. *Courtesy of Juan Colato.*

Silas Ballard and Edward Hegewald died overseas in France and by family request were reburied in Arlington National Cemetery. Ballard was the victim of a stabbing in a French town on October 27, 1918, while on shore leave from his navy ship. He was the first Redlands-area man to be reburied in the United States—on November 11, 1920—not long after reburials first started. Hegewald, a marine, was killed in action on November 2, 1918, in France and reburied in Arlington on October 20, 1921. Before the war, he was a bookkeeper for the E.M. Cope Commercial Company in Redlands, the same business that decorated its building with flags each time a draft train left town.

Four men claimed by Redlands were reburied in non-Redlands cemeteries. S. Benjamin Berry died of wounds received in action on July 22, 1918. Although claimed by Redlands, he was born in Unity, Maine, and had returned there before he enlisted, and it was there he was buried. The Unity American Legion Post is named for him, Benjamin Berry American Legion Post 50. Charles Raisner was a University of Redlands student when he was drafted on October 3, 1917. He was killed in action on September 30, 1918, and reburied in Corning, California.

Tragically, his brother, Howard Raisner, went down with the sinking of the SS *Tuscania* in February 1918. The American Legion Post in Corning is named for the two Raisner brothers, Raisner Post No. 45. Paul Smith entered World War I on April 4, 1917, with Redlands' Company G of the Seventh California Infantry, two days before war was declared. His death came during the Meuse-Argonne Offensive in France about September 26, 1918. He was reburied in the Banning, California cemetery. Less is known about Howard Thornton, but he was drafted on October 3, 1917, and served in a machine gun company in France, where he was

Ben Berry's Redlands High School graduation photograph, 1914, from the 1919 *Makio*.

killed in action around October 2, 1918. His reburial took place in Cerritos, California.

Two other men died overseas, John L. Moore (died of wounds received in action) and Roy Whiteside (killed in France), but no data has surfaced about exact dates and location of their burials. Whiteside was with the Canadian army.

GOLD STAR PILGRIMAGES

Ten Redlands families decided to leave their sons in American cemeteries in Europe. One man, Michael Stanley Jennings, died of the flu while on a troop transport ship crossing the Atlantic and was buried at sea.

Several leaders of the day pushed for the idea of leaving men's bodies overseas, including General Pershing (head of the U.S. military in Europe

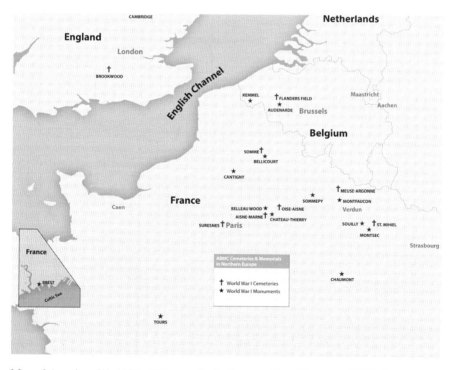

Map of American World War I Cemeteries in Europe. *Adapted from map* ABMC Cemeteries & Monuments in Northern Europe *with World War II Monuments and Cemeteries removed; courtesy of the American Battle Monuments Commission.*

Meuse-Argonne American Cemetery, Romagne, France. *Courtesy of the American Battle Monuments Commission.*

during World War I) and former president Theodore Roosevelt, who left his son Quentin buried overseas. The feeling was that the men should be buried where they fell with their comrades, but it also made a political statement to Europe that America had sacrificed for them. The over thirty thousand men buried in the eight American World War I cemeteries overseas certainly makes an impressive statement even today, including the over fourteen thousand in the Meuse-Argonne American Cemetery in Romagne, France.

No matter why a family left their deceased family member in Europe, they could not easily visit his grave. Men killed in action or who died of wounds shortly after battle had to be buried immediately and usually close to the fighting. Bodies were initially buried in cemeteries that were not their final resting places. The large World War I American cemeteries in Europe were not created until several years after the war ended. This caused disinterring of bodies and reinterring at least once—if not more than one time—not a pleasant job and fraught with the danger of misidentification and loss of bodies. Warfare during World War I also meant some bodies disintegrated from explosions, causing difficulty in finding or identifying them.

Many women in the United States felt that widows and mothers needed an opportunity to visit the graves in Europe for closure, but financially many could not do so. Throughout the 1920s, political pressure was put on the U.S. government to develop a program to transport these women overseas at no cost so that they could visit the graves. These women were called Gold Star mothers and widows, as a gold star meant they had lost their son or husband. Obviously, this meant many women would be eligible. The program was to be first class in transportation and travel, with costs covered from the woman's hometown and back (including train and ship travel, hotels and meals). Finally, in 1930, the first Gold Star Pilgrimages occurred, with the last in 1933. By this time, many of the mothers were reaching their sixties and seventies, while some had already passed away. If a widow had not remarried, she, too, could make a pilgrimage. Mothers and widows with men buried in Europe were asked if they wished to take one of these trips. Over 6,600 women out of the over 17,000 eligible eventually went. All were treated equally, except African American women, who traveled on segregated excursions, often on lesser-quality ships. The quartermaster corps organized these complicated trips, which involved moving women from different states to the right locations at the right time both in the United States and abroad.

But what about the widows and mothers of the ten Redlands-area men buried in Europe and the one who died at sea; did any of these mothers or widows go on pilgrimages? By 1930, when the first trips became available, five of the eleven mothers of the Redlands-area men buried in Europe had already died. Apparently, none of these men left widows. Amzi Jeffers, Manuel Marquez and Carl Tumlison lost their mothers before 1917, while Harry Lefler's mother died in 1922 and M. Stanley Jennings mother passed away during the 1920s. Jeffers, Marquez and Lefler are buried at the Meuse-Argonne American Cemetery in Romagne, France, while Tumlison is buried at the Suresnes American Cemetery in Suresnes, France. Jennings was buried at sea in the Atlantic, but his name is listed on the Tablets of the Missing at Suresnes American Cemetery.

Surprisingly, all but one of the six remaining eligible mothers related to Redlands-area men opted to go. Eulalia Flores, the mother of Teno Flores, turned down a trip, perhaps because English was not her native language and she was already seventy-two years old in 1930. Wounded, Flores died of pneumonia on November 6, 1918, in a hospital in France and was buried in St. Mihiel American Cemetery in Thiaucourt, France. The mothers of William Carson, Leonard Haws, Albert Simonds and Harold Tyrrell opted to go on a pilgrimage, and it appears that Harry Cook's mother may also have gone.

Two of the mothers, Josephine Tyrrell and Elsie Haws, went on the same ship in 1930, the SS *President Harding* (used for many of these pilgrimages). Most of the tours were about six weeks long round trip. Exactly when these two women left for Europe is currently unknown, but they returned from Cherbourg, France, on June 27, 1930, arriving at a New York port on July 5, 1930. Josephine Tyrrell (sixty years old and from Modesto, California) was the mother of Harold Tyrrell, a University of Redlands student who died in action or of his wounds on August 3, 1918, in France. Elsie Haws (sixty-one years old) lived in Highland. Her son, Leonard Haws, was killed in action on September 29, 1918, in the Meuse-Argonne Offensive. These women would probably have entrained from their hometown (as true of other women) and proceeded to the embarkation port, thence on a ship to France and on to Paris. After a few days in Paris, the women from a given ship were grouped together by cemetery where their sons were buried and taken to the cemetery for a visit that usually lasted about two days. This gave the women a chance to visit their sons' graves more than once. Then they returned to Paris for several more days, on to the port and back to the United States, where they were again entrained for their trip home. Tyrrell was buried in the Aisne-Marne American Cemetery in Belleau, France, while Haws is in the Meuse-Argonne American Cemetery in Romagne, France.

Two more mothers of Redlands-area men sailed to Europe in 1931, perhaps on the same trip. Josephine Cook (seventy-four years old with an address of 311 Summit Avenue, Redlands), mother of Harry Cook, apparently made at least one trip to France in the 1920s and another in 1930. She was listed as due to return on the Gold Star Pilgrimage of late June 1931 on the SS *President Harding* but did not get on the ship, perhaps traveling on her own later. Mary Simonds of Los Angeles (seventy-two years old) returned on the same ship and time that Josephine Cook was supposed to, leaving Cherbourg, France, on June 26, 1931, and arriving in New York by July 3, 1931. Cook made it through World War I only to die in a train wreck in France on December 5, 1918, after the war had ended. He was said to be the unofficial fiancé of Redlander Frances Willis, who would later become a U.S. ambassador. Albert Simonds, a marine, was killed in action on September 15, 1918, in France and buried in the St. Mihiel American Cemetery (the same one where Teno Flores lies). Cook was interred in Oise-Aisne American Cemetery in Fère-en-Tardenois, France.

No Redlands-area mothers went on 1932 pilgrimages, but Mary E. Carson of Redlands (seventy-six years old and living at 224 Sonora Street, Redlands) went on one of the last ones in 1933. She left Redlands on June

LEAVE TONIGHT FOR LONG TRIP

Gold Star Mothers Will Go to France to Visit Graves of Sons

Headline about Ollie Guin and Mary Carson's Gold Star Pilgrimage Tour, from the June 1, 1933 *Redlands Daily Facts*.

1, 1933, along with Ollie Guin (Mrs. Ollie Guin, 1007 Webster Street, fifty-seven years old), both from Redlands. Ollie Guin returned to Redlands six weeks later, on July 12, while Mary Carson stopped in Ohio to visit her son George. They sailed on the SS *President Harding* but this time left from Le Havre, France, on June 29, 1933, and returned to New York by July 7, 1933. About two weeks of their trip took place in France. Mary Carson's son, William Carson, was a marine and died of his wounds on July 19, 1918. His burial was in the Oise-Aisne American Cemetery where Cook is interred. Ollie Guin's son, William Guin, had registered and gone into the service from Texas, but she lived in Redlands at the time of her pilgrimage. Guin was her eldest son of thirteen children and died on the same day that Carson did, July 19, 1918, but was buried in Aisne-Marne American Cemetery, where Tyrrell rests.

Mrs. Guin was interviewed on the day she returned from France, July 12, 1933, by a *Facts* reporter who gave the following account of her trip:

William Carson's grave marker in Oise-Aisne American Cemetery, Fère-en-Tardenois, France. *Courtesy of the American Battle Monuments Commission.*

Not only were they given plenty of time to visit the graves of their sons, but they were taken on a wonderful sight seeing trip through the war country. All their expenses were paid by the government. "I have traveled so long, almost constantly for all that time, and seen so much that I am completely worn out and some what confused, but it was all wonderful," Mrs. Guin said this morning.

The Gold Star Pilgrimages were viewed as a success by those who went and proved well organized in their planning and implementation. Many women expressed relief that the cemeteries were well kept and the graves in good condition. The comments of many women matched those of Ollie Guin of Redlands that it was "all wonderful."

Death in Service within the United States

Thirteen men and one woman from the Redlands area died in service during World War I never having left the United States. Those who died within the country were usually sent back to their hometown for burial within a week of their death. Six Redlands men died of the flu and were buried in Hillside Memorial Park: James Backus, George Corwin, Banford Long, Dean Nethaway, Robert Owen (probably buried in Hillside) and Paul Sawyer. Edgar Putnam (died of heart failure) and Willard Best (died from a broken neck) were also brought back to Hillside Memorial Park for burial. Five additional deaths of Redlands men and women in service within the United States resulted in burials scattered from New York to California. Three of these died of the flu: Leland Rausch (buried in San Bernardino, California), Maybelle Wellman (buried in Alhambra, California, and later moved to Hillside Memorial Park, Redlands) and Jesse Wheaton (interred in Santa Ana, California). Additionally, Alan Bedell died of pneumonia (buried in Brooklyn, New York), and Perry Haddock was killed in a plane wreck in Texas (buried in San Diego, California). Not enough data on Harold Wright is currently known except that he died in a camp before May 11, 1918.

Redlands Memorials

By 1919, Redlands had started vigorously pursuing several ideas for World War I memorials for both veterans and those who died. Some projects materialized, but many simply disappeared.

The day after the armistice, November 12, 1918, work started to list the names of all Redlands-area veterans and those who died in service in the hallway of Redlands City Hall at Cajon and Vine Streets. On February 24, 1919, the list was complete, with at least eight hundred names. A gold star was affixed next to the name of each who had died in service. The list remained there for twenty years, until the building burned down in 1939.

Meanwhile, a committee, originally formed by the Business Men's Class of the Congregational Church and soon supported by the city trustees and chamber of commerce, began investigating what types of memorials the townspeople might want for veterans and for those who died in service. Mayor Archibald E. Brock (real estate and insurance work), Kirke H. Field (attorney) and S. Stillman Berry (chair of the committee, research zoologist and rancher) were members. Stillman Berry had lost his first cousin S. Benjamin Berry in World War I. Two popular memorials for those who died were envisioned. One was to plant redwoods in a tight grove in Sylvan Park with this type of tree selected due to its California connection and long life. Each person who died would have a tree planted with a bronze name plaque attached as the tree grew larger. Planting trees as memorials was popular after World War I, encouraged by the American Forestry Association. By February 24, the city had twenty-five redwoods ready to plant. On March 29, the *Facts* reported that the planting would probably occur on Memorial Day of that year. Memorial Day came and went, and nothing was mentioned. Nor does it appear that a grove of redwoods was ever planted in Sylvan Park. What happened to the trees? A redwood tree was planted in front of S. Stillman Berry's home on 1145 West Highland Avenue after the war in memory of his cousin, a tree that still stands today.

Another popular memorial idea was to install one or two bronze plaques outside Redlands City Hall's front doors with the names of those who had died in service during World War I. Did these plaques ever get installed? There is one bronze plaque created by the Redlands American Legion Post 106, and it hangs in the oldest mausoleum in Hillside Memorial Park. On it is listed thirty-five names of those who gave their lives, including that of Maybelle Wellman. One man was erroneously listed as dead although he survived the war. Elwood Emmett Whiteside, born in Redlands, was drafted on October 28, 1917, to Camp Lewis, Washington. He did not die until 1941. There was a Roy Whiteside of Redlands who served in the Canadian army and did die in World War I who is not mentioned on the plaque, perhaps the correct Whiteside. The history of when this plaque was created and how it ended up in the mausoleum, dedicated in 1928, is currently

Redwood tree planted in honor of S. Benjamin Berry, 1145 West Highland Avenue, Redlands, California. *Courtesy of Ann Deegan.*

unknown. It could not have been made earlier than May 1919, when the last man listed on the plaque died (Perry Haddock). All names listed, including the error with E.E. Whiteside's name, match those on the American Legion Charter List (American Legion Post 106), which was probably not created until after November 11, 1919, when charter membership may have ended.

American Legion Bronze Memorial Plaque in older mausoleum, Hillside Memorial Park, Redlands, California. *Courtesy of Ann Deegan.*

Debate continued on a fitting memorial to those who had served. A room was added to the Young Men's Christian Association building on East Citrus Avenue, similar to those that military men of World War I used for leisure in

American camps. Construction started in late March 1919. A pool table and a billiard table with cues and ivory balls were donated for the room.

By March 21, 1919, the redwood trees and bronze tablets appeared to be the main focus as expressed in the *Facts*:

> *The city trustees have decided not to take any steps for a permanent memorial for the boys who served in the world war for the present as all over the country there is a movement to not rush into memorials as has been done in the past and get things that in following years are not appreciated. It is felt that monuments and such things have been overdone, that practical memorials are the thing…. The city trustees will however as soon as possible order and place two bronze tablet at the entrance of the city hall with the names of those who gave their lives. There will also be planted in Sylvan Park sequoia trees dedicated to the boys.*

Redlands High School was collecting photos of its World War I veterans and those who died. In order to obtain as many as they could, they used the *Facts* of April 5, 1919, to solicit missing photos with a list of men's names. The photos were hung in a hallway at Redlands High School and were still being exhibited in October 1921. These photos do not seem to have survived.

A committee from the Contemporary Club, with a few city members, presented an idea for a museum on May 5, 1919, to the A.K. Smiley Public Library board. The women's committee consisted of Jennie E. Davis, Marion J. Fisher and Katharine J. Hunley. Mayor Brock and city engineer George Hinckley acted as Redlands City members. The committee wanted a new wing built on the library for an art gallery and museum run by library staff as reported in the *Facts* on May 5, 1919:

> *After discussion it was felt that the new building be erected, to be strictly fire proof, for an art gallery and museum purposes, a memorial to the soldiers and sailors who went to the war, memorial tablets for the heroes, literature and things connected with the great war being displayed there, as well as providing a museum for paintings. This building would be connected with the library but should be a separate structure. It was felt by all present that it would be a noble memorial. Mayor Brock agreed to appoint a special committee on the project.*

But plans were already in the works for a reference and children's wing at the library and that had first priority. Since no museum building was constructed, it is assumed that the idea fell through.

At some point, the Redlands American Legion Post 106 listed, framed and displayed in its building all the veterans names it knew of from the Redlands area (nearly nine hundred names) noting who had died in service. Included in this massive list were eleven women ranging from nurses to canteen workers. Eleven men in YMCA work, some overseas, were also included.

The town wanted to give a homecoming celebration to the veterans, but the men came home alone or in small groups throughout 1919 and then scattered, looking for jobs and moving on with their lives. At first, April 9, 1919, was the target date, but too few men were back. The town finally gave a thank-you party to the veterans on Armistice Day 1919 (November 11). A barbecue at noon, speeches and a football game between University of Redlands and Redlands High School provided the men a chance to celebrate the war's end. The veterans, when asked, had not wanted a parade in uniform. The American Legion threw a dance that evening.

Not until 1972, fifty-four years after the war's end, did another memorial appear in town that included the names of men who died in World War I. The Jennie Davis Park Memorial at Redlands Boulevard and New York Street, particularly developed to honor men who died in the Vietnam War,

Jennie Davis Park Memorial, Redlands Boulevard and New York Street, Redlands, California. *Courtesy of Ann Deegan.*

Frank Martinez grave marker in Veteran's Circle, Hillside Memorial Park, Redlands, California. *Courtesy of Ann Deegan.*

possesses names from other wars. Fifteen men who died in service in World War I appear on tiles along this wall. Inadvertently, about twenty-five names were left off, including the one woman who lost her life.

In 2015, ninety-seven years after the start of World War I, a group decided to obtain and install missing markers in the Veterans Circle of Hillside Memorial Park in Redlands. It started with a need to mark the grave of the first man buried there, Frank Martinez (killed in action in France on October 23, 1918). While researching his information, it was found that other markers were missing, ranging from Civil War through World War I veterans. Montecito Memorial Park and Mortuary in Colton, California, provided the eight markers and engraving costs, and Ryan Gallagher engraved the markers. The city council of Redlands waived all fees, and the work of Elks Lodge 583 of Redlands and the East Valley Young Marines, coordinated by Sam Irwin, helped this to happen. The Memorial Day 2015 ceremony took place at the circle, with the new markers prominently visible.

Redlands followed many national trends in its memorials, came up with some of its own original ideas and strove to thank families of those who had died in service and the veterans who returned. It is interesting that debate after World War I often discouraged the building of monuments and markers in favor of planting trees or constructing practical buildings. However, one hundred years after the war's end, many of the trees are now gone and buildings torn down, while monuments, including bronze plaques, survive. The town actively supported the war effort and did not forget the men and women who served.

Conclusion

Redlands, a town of about ten thousand in 1917, sent over eight hundred men off to war whether by drafting or enlistment. Many went overseas to fight or support those in combat, while others remained in the United States to train and assist. Women of Redlands left town as nurses, clerical workers and in other capacities, growing in ways unimagined before the war. The homefront fought as well in such efforts as bond drives and Red Cross projects. Redlands participated and after the war did not forget those who had fought and died. A small town with a big heart worked in a larger world effort. We hope that the stories included in this book, out of the many that could be told, help us all to appreciate that time in history and the role Redlands played.

Table 1

REDLANDERS LOST IN SERVICE TO THEIR COUNTRY

NAME	DATE DIED	CAUSE OF DEATH	PLACE OF DEATH	BURIAL
Backus, James M.	Oct. 20, 1918	influenza/ pneumonia	Camp Bowie, TX	Hillside
Ballard, Silas M.	Oct. 27, 1918	stabbed (non-combat)	France	VA
Bedell, Alan T.	Feb. 24, 1918	pneumonia	Gerstner Field, LA	NY
Berry, S. Benjamin	July 22, 1918	DWRIA	France	ME
Best, Willard R.	April 15, 1918	broken neck	Camp Kearny, CA	Hillside
Buehler, Omer R.	Sept. 28, 1918	DWRIA	France	Hillside
Carson, William A.	July 19, 1918	DWRIA or KIA	France	O-A
Cook, Harry	Dec. 5, 1918	railroad accident	France	O-A
Corwin, George R.	Oct. 8, 1918	influenza/ pneumonia	Camp Morrison, VA	Hillside
Douglas, Arthur W.	July 9, 1918	KIA	France	Hillside
Flores, Teno	Nov. 6, 1918	wounded, died of influenza	France	S-M
Forker, Albert E.	Oct. 1, 1918	DWRIA	France	Hillside

NAME	DATE DIED	CAUSE OF DEATH	PLACE OF DEATH	BURIAL
Haddock, J. Perry	May 6, 1919	airplane crash	Texas	CA
Haws, Leonard A.	Sept. 29, 1918	KIA	France	M-A
Hegewald, Edward T.	Nov. 2, 1918	KIA	France	VA
Jeffers, Amzi H.	Sept. 26, 1918	KIA	France	M-A
Jennings, M. Stanley	Oct. 5, 1918	influenza/ pneumonia	On the Atlantic	at sea
Lefler, Harry S.	Sept. 28, 1918	KIA	France	M-A
Long, Banford B.	c. Oct. 25, 1918	influenza/ pneumonia	Fort B. Harrison, IN	Hillside
Marquez, Manuel	Oct. 17, 1918	KIA	France	M-A
Martinez, Frank	Oct. 23, 1918	KIA	France	Hillside
Moore, John L.	By Dec. 12, 1918	DWRIA	France?	Unsure
Nethaway, Dean B.	Oct. 7, 1918	influenza/ pneumonia	Camp Logan, TX	Hillside
Owen, Robert N.	Jan. 16, 1919	influenza/ pneumonia	Vancouver Barracks, WA	Hillside?
Pearson, Caleb W.	Oct. 5, 1918	DWRIA or KIA	France	Hillside
Pray, Joseph	July 29, 1918	KIA	France	Hillside
Putnam, Edgar Fay	Oct. 7, 1917	heart failure	San Diego, CA	Hillside
Raisner, Charles C.	Sept. 30, 1918	KIA	France	CA
Rausch, Leland C.	Sept. 29, 1918	influenza/ pneumonia	Philadelphia, PA	CA
Richardson, Ernest O.	Oct. 29, 1918	KIA	France	Hillside
Sawyer, Paul P.	Nov. 24, 1918	influenza/ pneumonia	San Pedro, CA	Hillside
Simonds, Albert C.	Sept. 15, 1918	KIA	France	S-M
Smith, Paul D.	Sept. 26, 1918	KIA	France	CA
Thornton, Howard A.	c. Oct. 2, 1918	KIA	France	CA
Tumlison, Carl M.	Sept. 21, 1918	DWRIA	France	Suresnes
Tyrrell, Harold H.	Aug. 3, 1918	DWRIA or KIA	France	A-M
Wellman, Maybelle	Oct. 15, 1918	influenza/ pneumonia	Bronx, NY	Hillside

Name	Date Died	Cause of Death	Place of Death	Burial
Wheaton, Jesse F.	Oct. 21, 1918	influenza/ pneumonia	Camp Lewis, WA	CA
Whiteside, Roy	c. July 1918	KIA?	France	Unsure
Wright, Harold B.	By May 11, 1918	accident/other	in camp	Unsure

Key:

DWRIA = Died from wounds received in action

KIA = Killed in action

A-M = Aisne-Marne American Cemetery, Belleau, France

M-A = Meuse-Argonne American Cemetery, Romagne, France

O-A = Oise-Aisne American Cemetery, Fere-en-Tardenois, France

S-M = St. Mihiel American Cemetery, Thiaucourt, France

Suresnes = Suresnes American Cemetery, Suresnes, France

REFERENCE LIST

Books

American Battle Monuments Commission. *American Armies and Battlefields in Europe: A History, Guide, and Reference Book*. Washington, D.C.: Government Printing Office, 1938. Available online at www.abmc.gov.

Barry, John M. *The Great Influenza: The Epic Story of the Deadliest Plague in History*. New York: Penguin Books, 2004.

Budreau, Lisa M. *Bodies of War: World War I and the Politics of Commemoration in America, 1919–1933*. New York: New York University Press, 2010.

Byerly, Carol R. *Fever of War: The Influenza Epidemic in the U.S. Army During World War I*. New York: New York University Press, 2005.

Dickinson, John. *The Building of an Army: A Detailed Account of Legislation, Administration and Opinion in the United States, 1915–1920*. New York: Century Company, 1922.

Gavin, Lettie. *American Women in World War I: They Also Served*. Niwot: University Press of Colorado, 1997.

Graham, John W. *The Gold Star Mother Pilgrimages of the 1930s: Overseas Grave Visitations by Mothers and Widows of Fallen U.S. World War I Soldiers*. Jefferson, NC: McFarland & Company, 2005.

La Letra (University of Redlands annual)

Makio (Redlands High School annual)

McClellan, Edwin N. *The United States Marine Corps in the World War*. Washington, D.C.: Government Printing Office, 1920.

Redlands City Directories

Schneider, Dorothy, and Carl J. Schneider. *Into the Breach: American Women Overseas in World War I*. New York: Viking Penguin, 1991.

Wilson, Bryant, and Lamar Tooze. *With the 364th Infantry in America, France and Belgium*. New York: Knickerbocker Press, 1919.

NEWSPAPERS

Los Angeles Times
Redlands Daily Facts
Redlands Daily Review
San Bernardino Sun
Trench and Camp (Camp Kearny, California newspaper 1917–18)
Vancouver Sun

WEBSITES

American Battle Monuments Commission (ABMC). abmc.gov. Names and burial locations for men buried overseas in World War I.

American Red Cross. redcross.org/about-us/history/red-cross-american-history/WWI. "World War I and the American Red Cross."

Find-A-Grave. findagrave.com. Names and burial information across the country.

Hillside Memorial Park, Redlands, CA. cityofredlands.org/qol/cemetery. Online list of burials

Library of Congress. Prints and Photographs Division, Washington, D.C. loc.gov/pictures.

National Archives and Records Administration (NARA).
National Personnel Records Center
Subsection Military Personnel Records (MPR) Center: (NPRC-MPR)
Twentieth-century military records from 1917. archives.gov/st-louis/military-personnel
1 Archives Drive, St. Louis, MO 63138

National Archives and Records Administration (NARA). catalog.archives. gov/id/533461. American Unofficial Collection of World War I Photographs, 1917–18.

U.S. Federal Census records. archives.gov/research/census.

U.S. World War 1 Draft Registration Cards, 1917–18. archives.gov/ research/military/ww1/draft-registration.

INDEX

ABOUT THE AUTHORS

Ann Cordy Deegan received her doctorate in textile history at the University of Maryland and minored in U.S. history, with her dissertation related to the American Civil War. She has taught at numerous universities over the last thirty years, including the University of Maryland, Kansas State University, Utah State University, the University of Redlands and the University of California at Riverside. Additionally, she has been a curator of history in private and public museums, including the San Bernardino County Museum in Redlands, California, as head of the history division. She does research, writing and publishing in areas of U.S. history, particularly the nineteenth and early twentieth centuries, and has numerous publications in professional and public journals.

Maria Carrillo Colato is associate archivist of special collections at A.K. Smiley Public Library and the Lincoln Memorial Shrine. She has a bachelor of arts in history from California State University–Fullerton and a master of arts from the University of California–Riverside in history with an emphasis in public history. At a young age, she became fascinated by California history and has been interested in the study of the past ever since. As a graduate student, Maria served as a museum intern with the National Park Service at Fort Donelson National Battlefield in Dover, Tennessee. She has worked in museums and special collections in Southern California since 2006.

Nathan D. Gonzales studied history at the University of the Pacific and University of California–Riverside, where he earned his doctorate in 2006. In addition to individual work creating numerous articles and programs about the history of Southern California and Redlands, he has coauthored three books about the Redlands area, including *Faithfully and Liberally Sustained: Philanthropy in Redlands* and Images of America: *Redlands*. Nathan serves A.K. Smiley Public Library as archivist and head of special collections, as well as curator of the Lincoln Memorial Shrine.

Since 2013, Don McCue has been the director of A.K. Smiley Public Library and its affiliated museum, the Lincoln Memorial Shrine. For the prior twenty-six years, he served as the library's archivist and head of special collections as well as curator of the Lincoln Memorial Shrine, the only museum in the West dedicated to Abraham Lincoln and the American Civil War. In that capacity, he honed his military research skills and authored the 2008 book *Treasures of the Lincoln Memorial Shrine*. A strong proponent of the importance of military history, he has visited all of the major World War I and II battlefields in western Europe and has organized and led several tours of Civil War sites and battlefields.

Visit us at
www.historypress.net
....
This title is also available as an e-book